Blueprint for Developing Conversational Competence:
A Planning/Instruction Model with Detailed Scenarios

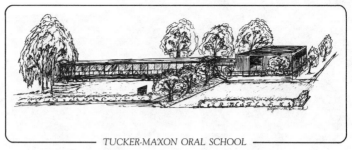

TUCKER-MAXON ORAL SCHOOL

Tucker-Maxon Communication Series

This series has grown out of the thinking and experience of the professional staff at Tucker-Maxon Oral School in Portland, Oregon. Each book blends current theory and actual practice at the school and provides practical and useable information for professionals and parents. *Blueprint for Developing Conversational Competence* is the first of the series.

1. Blueprint for Developing Conversational Competence: A Planning Instruction Model with Detailed Scenarios

A clear presentation of theory and procedures for developing the conversational ability of hearing-impaired children. Included are step-by-step procedures for evaluating, planning and carrying out instruction. A series of teaching scenarios guide the professional in implementing this effective approach.

2. Listening to Learn: A Parent's Guidebook for Hearing-impaired Children

This handbook provides parents with the essential steps necessary to develop effective communication with their children. Written by a team of outstanding professionals this book blends theory and practice in an eminently readable and practical fashion with many examples of actual conversational situations.

3. Developing Phonologic Speech

A compilation of activities designed to facilitate transfer of phonetic-level speech skills to the phonologic level. Also included is "teacher-friendly" information on acoustic phonetics as related to developing speech skills of hearing-impaired children.

4. Thinking Skills as factors in teaching communication strategies to hearing-impaired children.

5. Reading Skills and how to develop them for hearing-impaired children.

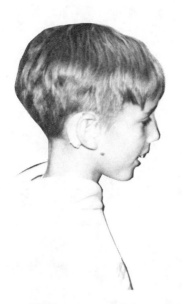

Blueprint for Developing Conversational Competence:
A Planning/Instruction Model with Detailed Scenarios

Patrick Stone, Director
Tucker-Maxon Oral School

Alexander Graham Bell Association for the Deaf
3417 Volta Place, N.W. Washington, D.C. 20007

Photography Credits:
All photographs were taken by
George Fortier, talented teacher, staff member
and contributing author.

Library of Congress cataloguing in publication data
Blueprint for Developing Conversational Competence:
A Planning/Instruction Model with Detailed Scenarios
Patrick Stone, Director
Tucker Maxon Oral School

Library of Congress catalogue card number 88-071410
ISBN 0-88200-164-7
©1988 by Alexander Graham Bell
Association for the Deaf
3417 Volta Place, N.W.
Washington, D.C. 20007

Printed in the United States of America
10 9 8 7 6 5 4 3 2 1

Dedication

to JoAnne

with love

Contents

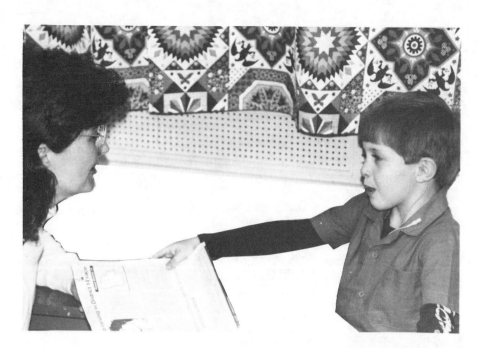

Preface

This text is a new look at an old problem. In it I have attempted to synthesize current research on the development of conversation by normally hearing children, teaching practices of the teachers with whom it is my pleasure to work, and my own experiences and values. I trust the outcome will be a coherent whole for the reader.

The problem of developing conversational competence in hearing-impaired children needs continual thought, revision and action. The "new look" in this book is the primacy given to conversation rather than language. It is clear to me that thinking in terms of developing the language of our students is outmoded and counterproductive. Rather, we need to focus on developing the conversational skills of our students. A by-product of this development is "straight language" that is usable and functional; in other words, conversational competence.

While the development of the strategies presented here was carried out at an oral school for hearing-impaired children, they have application to all hearing-impaired children, regardless of the method of communication chosen by their parents and teachers. Because of the developmental nature of the teaching strategies, they also have application for other groups of children who require a planned conversational development program.

This is a teacher's book. The strategies presented here were thought out, developed and refined by the very talented teachers at Tucker-Maxon. Their efforts are eloquent testimony to their dedication to their students and their profession. They are:

Deb Bervinchak
Dianne Blair
George Fortier
Pamela Fortier
Kelli Gehrs
Linda Goodwin
Connie Knepper
Catherine Lu
Gail Schiel
Margaret Smith
Christine Soland
Teresa Wolf

We are all grateful for the support of the parents who entrusted their children to us.

From 1981 to 1983 support for the development of the ideas presented here came from the Murdock Trust of Vancouver, Washington. Without the Trust's confidence and support this document would not have become a reality.
Valuable contributions were made to the project by Dr. Truman Coggins of the University of Washington. This book benefited greatly from suggestions made by Dr. Elizabeth Cole of McGill University. During the 1981-82 school year George Fortier of the Tucker-Maxon staff served as coordinator of the project. Their collective knowledge and wisdom added an important and powerful dimension.

The Board of Trustees of Tucker-Maxon Oral School provided encouragement, support and most of all, an environment which allowed for innovation.

To all of these people I express my sincere thanks.

Patrick Stone

1 Rationale

The instructional sequence and teaching strategies presented in this text are based on three important dimensions: 1) The nature and development of conversation; 2) The crucial role of context in language development; and 3) The limitations of most approaches currently used to teach language to hearing-impaired children.

Nature and Development of Conversation

Linguistic research during the past several years has clearly established that language acquisition by normally developing children is a result of conversational interaction (Snow and Ferguson, 1977; Waterson and Snow, 1978). Speaking of the development of language, Dore (1978) states, ". . . conversation itself is the immediate and primary context for acquisition." Dore continues, ". . . conversation is the most significant environment for learning language." Kretschmer and Kretschmer (1980) make an equally strong statement for the importance of conversation: "Children must learn language, that is, syntactic/semantic patterns, within the context of conversational exchanges. They learn language by engaging in conversations." Further support for the primacy of conversation as the vehicle of language learning comes from Bruner (1978): ". . . language acquisition occurs in the context of an 'action dialogue' in which joint action is being undertaken by infant and adult."

The importance of conversation is further underscored by the very early appearance of communicative exchanges between mothers and their infants. Several writers agree that these communication exchanges begin at birth. Bruner (1978) in reporting work done by MacFarlane, states that mothers attribute "intent to the cries, gestures, expressions and postures of newborns." This statement underscores the experience of everyone who has held a newborn. The drive to "talk to the baby" is universal.

During infancy the child begins to develop skills necessary for conversational competence. At first, adults appear to assume both roles in the conversational dyad, but with time, the child's maturing contributions become more and more important. Parents have increasing expectations for their children as conversational partners. Clark and Clark (1977) say, "Yawning and stretching may be enough at three months, but by eight months babbling is what really counts. And, by the age of one year or so, only words will do."

The earliest conversational skills that children acquire are the major elements of what can be called the STRUCTURE of conversation (specifically "initiating" and "turn taking"). For example, very young infants initiate contact with others by eye gaze and smiling. Similarly, the child's interest in social action games, such as peek-a-boo, suggests the developing notion of turn taking.

During this time, children begin to develop rudimentary knowledge of what can be called the FUNCTION of conversation. That is, children establish conversational topics by looking and/or pointing to an interesting object. When the parent responds to the child's topic introduction by saying something about it, he/she is maintaining the topic. Thus, the conversational cycle is established and continued with the parent establishing the turn-taking framework. Bruner (1975) reports that infants will maintain a topic chosen by their mothers as early as four months of age by following the mother's line of visual regard. Kretschmer (1981) reports a six-month-old child who had established "true conversations" with her mother.

The contributions of the child included smiles, body movements, eye gazes, grasping gestures and vocalizations at appropriate times in the conversational exchange.

Thus, long before conventional words and sentences (the FORM of conversation) appear, the child is establishing the basic STRUCTURE and FUNCTION of conversational discourse. It is this developing knowledge that the child uses to acquire further conversational abilities which ultimately become mature conversational competence.

Role of Context

The central role that context plays in the development of conversational skill is becoming increasingly apparent. Nelson (1981), in emphasizing the importance of context, states, ". . . the child does not build up language by analyzing its parts in terms of lexicon, syntax, phonology and pragmatics. Rather the child acquires the language according to contextually determined parts." Mishler (1979) states that understanding an utterance is "grounded in and dependent upon knowledge of the multiple contexts within which it appears." These authors agree that language is understandable and conversation is possible only because of listener and speaker ability to integrate all aspects of context during communication.

Keller-Cohen (1978) describes the four major types of context that effect language development as being situational, physical, social and linguistic. Situational context is made up of the gestures and actions of the participants in an interaction. Bates (1976) and Bruner (1974/75) postulate that gestures serve as the basis for the child's system of communication and become integral parts of messages when the child begins to talk. The salience of actions to the young child is reflected in the child's choice of lexical items and in the semantic relationships expressed by young children. (Nelson, 1981).

The physical context is made up of the perceptual properties of people and objects. Keller-Cohen points out that certain aspects of the people and objects with which the child interacts are the data used by the child to organize cognitive principles necessary to use and understand words.

Social context comprises three categories: the setting, the addressee and the interaction. Setting includes the physical features and sociocultural properties of the location. According to Keller-Cohen the child, "takes features of the setting into account in producing speech and in interpreting the utterances of others." The addressee component of social context takes into account the age and familiarity of the person being addressed and presuppositions concerning the knowledge, intentions and beliefs of that person. Clark and Clark (1977) point out that each speaker has expectations for what will happen in the conversation and uses appropriate social conventions when producing an utterance. The interaction component of social context includes the rules for securing attention, acknowledging the speaker, turn-taking and sustaining the interaction. Grice (1975) postulates that four maxims are necessary for sustaining interaction. They are: 1) be as informative as necessary; 2) be relevant; 3) be truthful; and 4) be appropriate. Competent conversationalists adhere to these rules during every conversational exchange.

The fourth context, the linguistic, is made up of the prior utterances produced by all of the speakers in an interaction. Ervin-Tripp (1977) and Cazden (1979) support the importance of linguistic context by pointing out that the particular semantic and syntactic constructions used in any given sentence are determined by all the utterances that have preceded it.

In summary, it can be seen that context in its many forms is both the foundation and framework of meaningful conversation. Prutting (1982) writes, ". . . what (the pragmatic literature has) in common is the centrality of context to the understanding of developmental pragmatics." The teaching procedures to be presented here are designed so that hearing-impaired children can acquire language within meaningful contexts. They are structured so that children can use context to acquire conversational competence.

Limitations of Current Approaches

In light of the growing knowledge of language acquisition, the popular approaches to teaching language to hearing-impaired children are seriously lacking in several vital dimensions. One serious deficiency is the lack of objectives and teaching strategies that directly address acquiring conversational competence. McKirdy and Blank (1982) state, "In large measure, discussions about language programs for the deaf have not concerned communication or the multiple roles that communication demands." Most, if not all, curricula emphasize acquisition of syntactic skills in drill and practice-type teaching situations, accompanied by the declared emphasis of having children practice their newly acquired syntactic skills throughout the day. This practice is in direct opposition to the research cited earlier which emphasizes the primacy of conversation as the most effective language learning environment. Kretschmer and Kretschmer (1978) state, "Unless the deaf child sees language within the context of dialogue, however, it is unlikely that he will ever learn it for functional use outside the classroom." The program to be described is based on the principle of using conversation as the primary strategy to obtain the goal of conversational competence.

In addition to approaching language instruction backwards, i.e., from syntax to conversation, most currently used programs ignore the vital role that the four aspects of context play in acquiring conversational competence. The situational, physical, social and linguistic contexts determine every utterance in a conversation. Isolated drill and practice on sentence forms ignore this reality and create in the child's mind a distorted sense of what language and communication are all about. Communication is not a didactic exercise, but a dynamic process involving two or more persons who want to share their thoughts and feelings. The procedures and strategies to be described emphasize the importance of all aspects of context and provide for their incorporation into the language acquisition process of hearing-impaired children.

Historically, language instruction for hearing-impaired children has relied to a large extent on the written form, based on the assumption that spoken and written English are identical. According to Kretschmer and Kretschmer (1986), ". . . it is critical to acknowledge that this assumption is false." Spoken conversation takes place on a face-to-face basis and conversational partners rely on all aspects of context to facilitate understanding. Written communication, on the other hand, takes place without benefit of face-to-face meeting. This places a burden on the writer to fill in all the context for the reader. To accomplish this, syntactic constructions are used in ways that differ from conversational constructions and various literary devices not found in spoken conversations are utilized to facilitate the readers comprehension. These differences mandate that instruction be clearly defined—conversational competence is obtained thru conversing; written language competence is obtained through writing. These assumptions are an integral aspect of the program to be described.

Another aspect of learning not often addressed in current research or general teaching practice is the generalization of learning. Too often educators assume that what has been learned in the classroom will carry over to everyday use. That this does not occur with regularity can be corroborated by every teacher of hearing-impaired children. This has been verified by the research of Guess, Keogh and Sailor (1978) and Stokes and Baer (1977). The latter authors refer to the assumption that classroom learning will automatically be used in other places and with other people as "train and hope." While there is much to be learned about generalization of learning, the program presented in this text begins to address this most important component of instruction.

Summary

The nature and development of conversation and the role that context plays in acquisition of conversational competence make it clear that most currently used programs are seriously deficient. The core of this deficiency lies in the implicit and explicit assumptions made about language and learning. The Planning/Instruction Model to be presented is based on the following principles:

1. Conversation is the optimal environment in which hearing-impaired children acquire conversational competence.
2. Acquiring conversational competence is best accomplished when instruction accounts for all aspects of context.
3. Spoken language and written language are different. Instruction in each area should be independent of the other.
4. Systematic instruction and planning for generalization of learning are essential for children to carry over classroom instruction to everyday living.

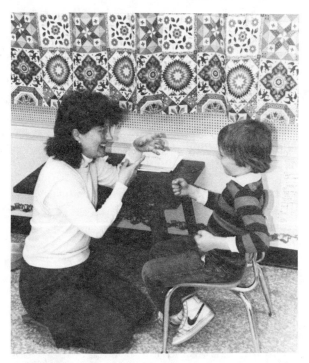

2 Conversational Framework

In order to facilitate instruction and provide a coherent model of conversation a "Conversational Framework" has been developed. This framework views conversation as having three components: Structure, Function and Form. The Structure of conversation is made up of initiating, turn-taking and ending. These are the components of conversation which are not meaning oriented, but rather, serve to manage the conversation. (Lund and Duchan, 1983) They correspond closely with the interaction component of social context as discussed by Keller-Cohen (1978). The Function of conversation is to share thoughts, feelings and ideas. Within conversation this is realized by introducing and maintaining topics. Speakers introduce and maintain topics by using the communicative intents of commenting, requesting, acknowledging and answering. (See Note 1, p. 26) Finally, the Form of conversation consists of the semantic, syntactic and morphologic constructions used by speakers.

Structure

Initiation is that aspect of conversation which serves to let another speaker know that the first speaker is interested in and/or available for a conversation. Clark and Clark (1977) refer to this as the summons-answer sequence. Initiation can be accomplished by simply moving closer to a prospective conversational partner, smiling or making eye contact. In most situations it is accompanied by a ritualized and routine verbal expression. Social encounters are settings containing all these elements:

Bob: Moving toward Betty, smiling and looking her in the eyes, says, "Haven't we met before?"

Betty: Smiling and shifting to face Bob responds, "I'm sure we have."
(A successful initiation by Bob and a friendly response by Betty.)

Teachers are familiar with this example of initiating by a seven-year-old:

Jane: Bursting into the classroom declares, "You know what?"

Miss J: "No, what?"
(Jane had made a successful initiation and the two are ready to begin discussion of a topic to be introduced by Jane.)

Additional initiation routines which appear with regularity are statements such as these:

"Hi honey, I'm home."
"How's everything?"
"Mom!"

Initiation is the first aspect of conversation to be utilized by infants. Smiling, crying and vocalizing are examples of the initiation strategies employed by infants (Bruner, 1978). Each is effective in its own way.

Initiating has important social implications. The age and status of the conversational partner plays a key role in the selection of the verbal routines used to initiate. For some partners an informal "How's it goin'?" is appropriate, while for others the more formal, "Good morning." is the initiating phrase of choice. Becoming a competent conversationalist requires appropriate use of a wide range of socially acceptable means of initiating conversation with a variety of individuals.

Turn-taking is the second dimension of the Structure of conversation. In the dialogues above, two important facets are present. First, Bob and Jane had to stop talking to allow their respective partners time to respond. Likewise, Betty and Miss Jones are required to wait until their partners are finished before speaking. In other words, overlapping of utterances is generally not acceptable in polite conversation. The second important facet of conversational turn-taking is that the gap between turns is brief so as to maximize efficiency. Speakers expect their conversational partner to respond to their utterance quickly.

Speakers often use one of a variety of verbal routines which serve the dual purpose of taking a turn and assuring the speaker that interest and understanding are continuing. Pertinent examples of these are:

> "Really!"
> "You're kidding."
> "Uh huh."

important for Deaf

A turn-taking strategy used by young children (and parents among others) is to repeat all or part of the previous utterance. This appears not only to serve a turn-taking role, but also as a means for the child to practice a linguistic construction. Playing peek-a-boo and other repetitive, social action games engaged in by parents and young children are important precursors to mature conversational turn-taking.

Ending conversation is accomplished by using one of the variety of verbal routines, e.g., "Good-bye," "See you later," etc. These ending rituals are often preceded by pre-ending routines such as, "Well, I really have to be going." or "Does that cover everything?" Typically young children do not formally end conversations, but merely turn or walk away when they perceive the coversation to be complete (Clark and Clark. 1977). As with initiating, different conversational partners and situations call for different types of closing rituals.

In summary, Initiation, Turn-Taking and Ending serve as the Structure of conversation. They are the foundation and framework upon which the later-emerging Function and Form of conversation are built. A major component of conversational competence is having a broad repertoire of verbal and non-verbal means of structuring conversational discourse, i.e., initiating, turn-taking and ending. This repertoire will be developed by hearing-impaired children only if they are given abundant opportunities to engage in and learn from meaningful conversation.

Function

The function of conversation is to share thoughts, feelings and information. This is accomplished by the complementary processes of Topic Introduction and Topic Maintenance. Speakers introduce topics by using the communicative intents of requesting and commenting. Topics are maintained by the communicative intents of answering, acknowledging, requesting and commenting.

Returning to Bob and Betty:

> **Bob:**   "Weren't you at the concert last night?"
> (Introducing topic by requesting information.)
> **Betty:**   "Yeah I was. That band was great."
> (Maintaining topic by answering, followed by a comment.)

Using a comment to introduce a topic is utilized by Jane with her teacher, Miss Jones.

> **Jane:**   "My dog had puppies last night."
> **Miss J:**   "Oh how nice. How many puppies did she have?"
> (Miss Jones maintains the topic by acknowledging and then requesting more information.)

Young children learn to introduce topics long before they are using words or sentences (Clark and Clark, 1977). Foster (1983) reports children giving " . . . indication of the object of interest" (topic introduction) as early as five months. Once an infant has established eye contact with the parent (initiation), s/he might look at/or point to a favorite toy and babble. The parent responds to this topic introduction by handing the child the toy and saying, "Here you go.

You love that teddy bear don't you?" Here the infant's topic introduction consisted of a request for an object by looking and babbling. The parent maintained the topic and answered the request by handing the teddy bear to the child followed by appropriate comments.

A second type of request is requesting an action. An example familiar to all parents is the young child holding out his/her hands and saying, "Up. Up." The parent's answer to this request is to do the picking up. The first topic introduction strategies mastered by children are those of requesting objects and actions by using movement, eye gaze, gestures or gestures accompanied by vocalizing.

The third type of request to emerge is that of requesting information (Clark and Clark, 1977). Early requests for information may be yes/no questions marked by rising intonation e.g. "Go-bye-bye?" or WH-questions such as "Where daddy go?" As the child gains motor skills and is able to do more for him/herself requests for information come to dominate the young child's conversation. The continual use of "What's that?" and "Why?" are requests for information familiar to all parents and teachers.

Maintaining topics requires producing utterances that are contingent upon prior utterances and that relate to the general concern of the topic under discussion (Foster, 1982). Foster reports that children under two years are able to perform the first of these tasks, i.e., contingent utterances, but are unable to produce a series of utterances related to a central topic. Foster goes on to point out the fundamental role played by adult-child routines, e.g., feeding time, bath time, going to bed time etc., through which the child learns the cultural expectations of conversation. These routines provide the framework within which children can exhibit an increasing amount of planning of their conversational contributions. In other words, the many routine exchanges between children and their caregivers serve as contextual support for the child as s/he learns how to maintain a topic. With time and practice the child gains mastery of the routines and eventually is able to structure conversation so that all utterances are contingent and relate to the topic at hand.

To maintain topics speakers use the communicative intents of commenting and requesting as well as answering and acknowledging. Answering is the appropriate response to any of the requests discussed above. Answers and acknowledgements may be non-verbal, verbal or a combination of both. Acknowledgements serve to let the conversational partner know that a comment has been heard and understood.

Bob and Betty continue their conversation:

> **Betty:**   "His last movie was great."
> **Bob:**   "Yeah. I hear his new one will be even funnier."
> (Acknowledgement followed by a comment.)

A specialized type of request that serves a topic maintenance function is that of requesting clarification. This strategy is used by all speakers, but has particular import for hearing-impaired children. They are likely to encounter many speakers who for various reasons are difficult to understand and they will often be in environments which interfere with efficient communication. Learning to request clarification politely and accurately is critical to the smooth flow of conversation.

To return to Bob and Betty:

> **Bob:**   "Last summer I went to Moscow for two weeks."
> **Betty:**   "You were where?"
> (A specific request for clarification.)

In the classroom Jane makes a generalized request for clarification:

> **Miss J:**   "Are they male or female?"
> **Jane:**   "What?"
> (A generalized request for clarification.)
> **Miss J:**   "Do you have girl or boy puppies?"
> **Jane:**   "Oh. One is a boy and . . . "

These two examples point out a significant aspect of clarification requests, namely, the specificity of the request. It is important for hearing-impaired children to learn to be as specific as possible in requesting clarification. The type of request made by Betty lets Bob know exactly which part of the message was not understood. This efficiency facilitates smooth conversation.

Following is a list of the communicative intents used by speakers to introduce and maintain topics:

Topic Introduction
Request for object
Request for action
Request for information
Comment

Topic Maintenance
Answer
Acknowledgement
Request for clarification
Request for object
Request for action
Request for information
Comment

Topical Cohesion

When engaged in conversation speakers use a number of linguistic devices which serve to tie utterances together. Halliday and Hasan (1976) identify several such linguistic devices. Three of particular importance are use of articles, pronouns and ellipsis.

Articles serve to identify whether the following noun is old information, i.e., has been referred to earlier in the conversation or is present in the immediate physical context; or whether it is new information not previously identified in the conversation or environment. Use of the definite article, "the" lets the listener know that the noun which follows is old information that has been referred to earlier in the conversation or is present in the immediate area. This greatly facilitates the listener's comprehension. On the other hand use of the indefinite article "a" (or "an") refers to new information and informs the listener that the following noun has not been referred to earlier in the conversation. The articles serve an important conversational function by helping the listener identify the status of information—old or new—and thus serve to help tie successive utterances together in a meaningful whole.

Pronouns are also used to refer to old information, whether the information has been spoken of previously or is in the immediate environment. They can substitute for single words, sentences and even paragraphs. In this way they speed the flow of conversation and contribute greatly to conversational efficiency and effectiveness.

Ellipsis: A third linguistic device which contributes to conversational cohesion is ellipsis, or the omission of information already known to the listener and therefore redundant. For example, when a speaker responds to the question, "Where did you get the great tan?" with "In Mexico," the questioner fills in the omitted information. To reply with, "I got my tan in Mexico" would be conversationally redundant. Ellipsis can carry over through several conversational turns around a topic. In this way it serves to facilitate the smooth flow of conversation.

Articles, pronouns and ellipsis also further the efficiency of conversation by reducing the length of utterances. Using "the" when referring to known information eliminates the need for re-establishing the referent. Pronouns accomplish the same purpose by allowing speakers to substitute one word for several words, sentences or even paragraphs. Ellipsis contributes to conversational efficiency by eliminating the production of information that would be redundant.

Effective and efficient use of articles, pronouns, and ellipsis will do much to further the ability of hearing-impaired children to engage in conversation. Because they are conversational cohesion devices they can best be learned within meaningful conversation.

Extended Turns

Not all conversational turns are made up of one or two sentences. Many conversational utterances are very long and have an internal structure all their own. Conversations are replete with these extended turns. The major types are narratives, explanations, directions and descriptions. Each of these are used to comment, answer, acknowledge or request.

Bob and Betty are still visiting:

> **Betty:**   "Tell me how it is that you come to be living here."
> **Bob:**   "Well, when I graduated from college . . ."
>   (An answer that takes the form of a narrative.)

Miss Jones asks for information that results in a description:

Miss J: "Tell me what they look like."
Jane: "One is brown all over with white feet and one has
             white only on one foot and . . ."
             (An answer that is a description.)

Later in this conversation Jane provides a narrative:

Jane: "I'll tell you what happened. We were all eating dinner
             when we heard Buffy, the mother dog, scratching at
             the door. Then . . ."

From these examples it is evident that extended turns play a significant role in conversation. Hearing-impaired children need to have a great deal of practice with each if they are to master them and become competent conversationalists.

Unfortunately, except for narratives, there is little or no data on the development or structure of extended turns. Applebee (1978) describes six stages in the development of narrative structure:

- *Stage 1—"Heaps":* a series of unconnected utterances
- *Stage 2—Sequences:* events have an arbitrary sequence
- *Stage 3—Primitive Narratives:* a collection of complementary events organized around a central situation
- *Stage 4—Unfocused chains:* incidents lead from one to another, but linking attributes shift
- *Stage 5—Focused chain:* sequencing and relating to a central idea are joined
- *Stage 6—Narrative:* a complete, well-formed story

Applebee reports that the majority of stories by four and five-year-olds are of the "focused chain" and "narrative" types. This early acquisition is corroborated by Stein and Glenn (1979) who report that children as young as five are aware of basic narrative organization and use it to create and comprehend stories.

Several writers (Rumelhart, 1975; Mandler and Johnson, 1977; Stein, 1978; Sadow, 1982) have described the structure of narratives. This work can be summarized by stating that a well-formed narrative includes:

1. A setting which establishes the main character(s) and the time, place and social context.
2. A statement which identifies a problem to be solved or a goal to be attained. This is accompanied by stating the emotional state/response of the characters.
3. The sequence of actions taken by the characters. These are the episodes of the story. (A variety of time and causal connectors are an important component of competence.)
4. An ending which states the solution or attainment of the goal along with the emotional response of the character(s).

This quality of research data is not available for the other extended turns. However, after examining several samples of each, the following tentative guidelines are offered. An adequate explanation requires at least the following:

1. Opening with a statement that clearly defines the expected outcome of the activity;
2. Listing the materials and equipment necessary; and
3. Describing the appropriate actions in proper sequence using a variety of verbs and time connectors.

Returning to Jane and Miss Jones:

Miss J: "How did you make a bed for all those puppies?"
Jane: "First we got a big box and some old blankets. Then we cut off the lid and one of the sides. After that we put in some old blankets."

Adequate giving of directions requires at least the following:

1. Beginning the sequence at a point which is clear and known to the listener;
2. Using a variety of locative terms and phrases, e.g., down the hall, turn right at the corner, cross the street, go five blocks, etc.; and
3. Using a variety of time connectors, e.g., when you see the store, after that, before the intersection, etc.

Returning to Bob and Betty:

Betty: "I can tell you how to get there. Do you know how to get on Interstate 5 going north?"

Bob: "Yeah."

Betty: "O.K. Once you're on it go to the Mill Plain exit and turn right. Go down Mill Plain until you see a McDonalds. At the first stop light after that turn left. It's the fourth house on the right."

The final extended turn to be considered is that of describing. An adequate description requires the following:

1. Relating only the distinctive features of the object or person, and omitting extraneous information already known to the listener;
2. Using relative clauses and "with" phrases to amplify the description; and
3. Using a rich variety of description for interest.

Acquiring competence with each extended turn has important implications for conversational competence and equally important implications for reading skill. Each extended turn plays a vital role in spoken and written communication. Being able to relate and comprehend stories during conversation is the foundation of narrative competence which ends by being able to read short stories and novels with understanding and enjoyment. Modern reading theory places great emphasis on the importance of the cognitive schemata readers bring to the task. The most fundamental of these schemata when reading fiction is narrative structure.

The ability to provide and understand simple explanations during conversation is a precursor to reading and understanding text books. Text books are merely long and detailed explanations of social and physical phenomena. Comprehension begins with an understanding of the structure of explanation which is developed through conversational exchanges.

Descriptions and directions are important components of fiction and non-fiction. Developing adequate skills at a conversational level lays the groundwork for their utilization during reading.

The overall low achievement of hearing-impaired readers is well documented. A significant factor contributing to this problem is a breakdown in their ability to handle these extended turns within conversation. Therefore, instruction of hearing-impaired children must provide for their acquisition.

To summarize, the Function of conversation, i.e., sharing thoughts, feelings and ideas, is made up of the processes of topic introduction and topic maintenance. Each of these is accomplished by a variety of communicative intents, i.e., requesting, commenting, answering and acknowledging. Utterances which carry out these intents may be single words, single sentences or extended turns. Competent conversationalists utilize a number of linguistic cohesion devices which serve to tie successive utterances together. To acquire facility with the function of conversation and all its dimensions hearing-impaired children must have extended and mainingful opportunities to engage in conversation.

Form

The Form of conversational discourse is made up of the words, phrases and sentences that are spoken. The most productive means of describing this component is to use semantic categories for one-word utterances; semantic relationships for two and three-word utterances; and syntactic and morphologic rules to describe further development. This does not imply that these categories have psychological reality for the child, only that they are useful ways of describing linguistic development.

The one-word utterances of children can be described as being made up of nine semantic categories. These semantic categories with examples are listed below.

- Existence—"This", "That", Labels for objects and persons
- Non-Existence—"No", "Allgone"
- Recurrence—"More"
- Rejection—"No"
- Denial—"No"
- Action—"Go", "Help"

- Locative action—"Up"
- Possession—"My", Names of persons
- Attribution—"Hot", "Dirty"

Fifteen semantic relationships are expressed in two-word utterances. These are combinations of the one-word categories listed above with some additions:

- Existence: "That one."
- Non-Existence: "No ball." "Allgone milk."
- Recurrence: "More juice."
- Denial: "No do."
- Rejection: "No bed."
- Agent and Action: "Mommy go."
- Action and Object: "Push car."
- Agent and Object: "Daddy car."
- Action and Location: "Go store."
- Entity and Location: "Ball here."
- Attribute and Entity: "Big boy."
- Experiencers and Process: "You think."
- Process and Entity: "Want ball."
- Action and Recipient: "Give mommy."
- Action and Instrument: "Sweep broom."

These two-word utterances give way to three-word semantic relationships. Three-word utterances are created by combining two of the two-word relationships and deleting the common word. For example "Mommy go store." is a product of combining "Mommy go." with "Go store." and deleting the word that is common to each. Some of the most common are listed below:

- Agent and Action and Object: "Daddy hit ball."
- Agent and Action and Location: "Mommy go store."
- Action and Object and Location: "Put ball here."
- Experiencer and Process and Object: "I want cookie."

Moving beyond the three-word stage involves refining sentences and increasing their complexity. The primary refinements are made up of adding function words, e.g., in, on, a, the, is, was, has, do, etc., and grammatical morphemes, e.g., -ing, -s (plural and possessive), irregular past tense, regular past tense, etc. It is of interest that ten of the fourteen earliest learned function words and grammatical morphemes have to do with the verb phrase.

The earliest increases in complexity are made up of producing negative sentences and question forms. According to Clark and Clark the earliest negatives are formed by adding a negative element (no or not) before or after a statement as in "No go store.", "Not go bed.", or "Drink milk no." The next stage is characterized by adding "don't" and "can't" to "no" and "not" and inserting one of them into a sentence in the appropriate location. The final stage brings use of additional negatives such as "didn't" and "won't".

Children go through a similar progression in the development of question forms (Clark and Clark, 1977). The earliest questions are a result of adding appropriate intonation to affirmative statements producing yes/no questions such as "Baby drink?", "See ball?", or "Go bye-bye?" At this stage children also ask "Where" and "What" questions by prefacing statements with one or the other. The next stage is characterized by longer yes/no questions that are still marked only by intonation, e.g., "You want go store?" or "You can't eat?" WH-questions now include "Why" in addition to "Where" and "What". However, in neither type of question are the subject and verb inverted, e.g., "What the boy do?" or "Why mommy go?" In the next stage the subject and verb are inverted and the auxiliary is present in yes/no questions, e.g., "Can you play?" However there are still mistakes with tense and number suffixes on the auxiliary. "Which" and "How" are added to the types of WH-questions, but the subject and verb are still not inverted. This produces sentences such as "How he do that?" and "Which one I should take?" The next stage brings correct auxiliary and subject placement.

Shortly after children begin forming questions and negatives they begin combining ideas in one sentence to form complex sentences which increases the efficiency of conversation. Complex sentences are formed to link two or more ideas of equal value (coordination); to restrict or modify the verb phrase (adverbial clause); to restrict or modify one of the noun phrases (relative clause); and to insert ideas by filling an empty position in a sentence (noun clause, infinitive and participle).

Linking two ideas of equal value in a sentence is usually accomplished by using the conjunctions "and", "but" and "or". These conjunctions can join a variety of forms which include:

- Two noun phrases:
  "Mary and Jim won the race."
  "They could choose a trophy or plaque."
- Two verb phases:
  "Her puppy ran and hid."
  "He didn't bark or growl."
- Two clauses:
  "Mom likes to dance but she doesn't like rock and roll."

Relative clauses are used to modify or restrict a noun phrase. Some examples are:

"She married the man that she met in college.
"Her uncle who won the lottery gave them a new car."

Not all relative clauses are marked by the use of a relative pronoun. For example the first sentence above could be said and understood if "that" were left out. The first relative clauses that children use are those that modify an empty noun (one, thing, kind) in the object position.

"See the one I got!"

These first relative clauses do not contain a relative pronoun.

The first relative pronoun to be used is usually "that" again modifying the object noun phrase:

"I got the teacher that I wanted."

Children begin to use "who" and "which" as relative pronouns after they are using them in questions.

"He's the one who doesn't give homework."

Children place relative clauses at the end of sentences before they learn to embed them to modify the subject noun phrase.

Adverbial clauses modify verb phases and are used to specify time (when, before, after, until), causal (because, so, since) and conditional (if) relationships. Adverbial clauses can precede or follow the main clause:

> "He played hard after putting in a full day."
> "Before Mary left for school she ran five miles."
> "She's very happy because it's her birthday."
> "If it rains again I'll scream."

Adverbial clauses which appear at the end of the sentence and those which maintain the time order are learned first.

The three kinds of complements, infinitives, participles and noun clauses, function as noun phrases in the subject or object position. Some examples are:

> "Jogging is my favorite activity." (Participle)
> "My wife likes to walk." (Infinitive)
> "I wish that I could run faster." (Noun clause)
> "What I want is a trophy." (Noun clause)

Each of the complements replaces the noun "something" and are usually marked by "-ing", "to", "that" or "what".

The earliest complements used by children are infinitives with the main verb being "want" and "have" as in:

> "I 'wanna' (want to) buy it."
> "I 'hafta' (have to) go."

Following this other main verbs are used with the infinitive form where the subject of the main verb and infinitive are the same. Later appearing are infinitives that have different subjects for the main verb and infinitive:

> "He wanted me *to go sking*."

The earliest appearing noun clause complements are those introduced by "that" and, as with all other complex sentences, they initially appear at the end of the main clause:

> "I think that I will go sailing instead."

Later appearing noun clauses are introduced by "where" "what" and "why":

> "But I don't know where the boat is."
> "What I don't understand is why he left it home."

Children begin to combine ideas within sentences at the age of two-and-a-half or three. Complete mastery of all the ways to form complex sentences takes eight to ten years. In general forms that contain consistent grammatical markers and that appear after the main clause are the first to develop. Forms that use grammatical markers inconsistently and that interrupt the main clause are more difficult to master.

A description of the development of semantic, syntactic and morphologic usage is included in the Stages of Conversational Development which appears in the section on Selecting Objectives.

Summary

Conversation is a multi-faceted activity with several important strands:

1. Structure: the routine social conventions upon which effective conversation depends:
   - Initiating
   - Turn-taking
   - Ending
2. Function: the reason for conversation, i.e., the sharing of thoughts, feelings and ideas
3. Form: the surface of conversation, i.e., the semantic, syntactic and morphological constructions

The components of conversation are best learned within conversation itself. The Planning/Instruction Model to be presented is based on conversation as the primary instructional strategy and conversational competence as the ultimate goal. Before discussing the Model, it is necessary to introduce the concept of Conversational Scenarios.

The Conversational Framework presented on the following page organizes these ideas.

CONVERSATIONAL FRAMEWORK		
STRUCTURE	**FUNCTION**	**FORM**
• Initiation	• Topic Introduction Requests Comments	• Semantics
		• Syntax
• Turn-Taking	• Topic Maintenance Answers Acknowledgements Requests Comments	• Morphology
• Ending		

Note 1

Dore (1978) includes our initiating, turn-taking and ending in his category of "regulative conversational acts." The intents we include in the Function category Dore labels "content conversational acts." We have chosen to group them as we have because the Structure items do not carry meaning, but are the mechanics which govern conversation. The Function items, on the other hand, do carry the intent of the speaker, i.e., requests, comment, answer or acknowledge, and thus are central to the meaning of each utterance.

Clark and Clark (1977) describe conversations as having two types of structure—hierarchical and local. Their hierarchichal structure corresponds closely with our Structure category while their local structure corresponds to our Function and Form. That is, conversation has a hierarchical structure that grows out of the purpose and type of conversation. This determines the opening, the exchanges and ending. The local structure refers to each of the sentences uttered and is determined by the agreement between speakers to respond to the intent and content (Function and Form) of each utterance.

These perspectives and our own experience using the Conversational Framework as a teaching guide persuade us of its efficacy.

3 Conversational Scenarios

Conversational scenarios are the primary strategy for facilitating the acquisition of conversational competence by hearing-impaired children. This section will explain scenarios and give several examples and is followed by information on how to develop role-playing ability in hearing-impaired children.

Explanation and Examples

Scenarios are role-playing situations which contain appropriate dialogue. They are planned by the teacher and presented to the child in such a way that a realistic conversation takes place between teacher and child. The child's part in the conversation requires the use of a specific conversational skill which has not been mastered. Acquiring this skill is the teacher's objective.

In the following example, the teacher has determined that her eight-year-old student needs to improve his ability to include a well-formed setting statement in his conversational narratives. (The teacher is identified as T, the student is S.)

> **T:** "Let's pretend that you live close to school. You walk to school each morning. One morning you are coming to school and it starts to rain. You don't want to get wet so you run to school. But, when you get here you can't find your homework. You must have lost it. You tell me what happened."
>
> **S:** "O.K."
>
> **T:** "Who are you?"
>
> **S:** "Me. You are the teacher."
>
> **T:** "Let's start."
>
> **S.** (Goes to classroom door and pretends to come in.) "Good morning."
>
> **T:** "Hi, how are you?"
>
> **S:** "I can't find my homework."
>
> **T:** "What happened?"
>
> **S:** "I lost it. It's raining."
>
> **T:** "Well, I guess you'll have to do it over."

This student attempted to tell his story, but the setting was incomplete. Teaching objectives and instruction will focus on improving the setting statement. Specific procedures will be discussed in the Planning/Instruction Model.

Here is an example with a five-year-old. The teacher has determined that her student is ready to learn to request using "and" to join two nouns:

T: "Today, let's pretend that you are at home and you're very hungry. Your mom has just made a cake. You want a piece and you want some ice cream, too. I'll be your mom and you be yourself. This will be the kitchen and you come in.

S: "O.K."

T: "Who am I?"

S: "Mom."

T: "Right. Who are you?"

S: "Me"

T: "Right. And where are we?"

S: "At home."

T: "O.K. Let's start. You come into the kitchen."

S: "Mom."

T: (As Mom) "What?"

S: "I'm hungry. I have cake ice cream."

T: "Well, I don't know if you can have both."

S: "Cake?"

T: "All right, I'll cut you a piece."

In this case the student came close to the appropriate language. Appropriate intervention strategies will be discussed later.

These examples demonstrate the essential elements of conversational scenarios. They are:

1. The situation and topics are familiar to the student.
2. The teacher makes sure that the student understands the situation before beginning.
3. As the dialogue proceeds there is a conversational need for the targeted conversational skill to arise.
4. The teacher does not tell the child what to say, rather the situation and conversation bring about a need for use of the targeted skill.
5. The situation and conversation are carried to a logical conclusion.

Scenarios are also used to have children develop skill with the other extended turns. In the following example the teacher has determined that her twelve-year-old student needs additional skill with giving directions:

T: "This time I want you to pretend that you are going to have a birthday party at your house. You need to tell me how to get to your house from school. It's before school and I am working at my desk. You come in to tell me about the party.

"Do you have any questions?"

S: "The party is at my house?"

T: "Yes."

S: "O.K."

T: "Let's start."

S: (Gets up and moves to door and pretends to come in.) "Good morning."

T: "Hi, how are you?"

S: "Fine. Tomorrow is my birthday party at home. Can you come?"

T: "Well, I think so. Can you tell me how to get there?"

S: "Yes. Go up the street very far. Turn. Turn again. My house is brown and white."

T: "How far up the street should I go? What's the name of your street?"

S: "I live on 72nd Avenue."

T: "Oh, O.K. Thank you."

S: "You're welcome."

This student's ability to give directions needs improvement. The procedures used by the teacher to accomplish this will be discussed later.

The following scenario was designed to help a student acquire the ability to introduce a topic with a comment that has a relative clause to specify information:

T: O.K. Let's pretend that yesterday a doctor came to our room to watch you and the other children. He wanted to find out about hearing-impaired children and what they do in school. Then, last night you went to the store with your mom and you saw that doctor. You talked to him and he remembered you."

S: "I talked to the doctor?"

T: "Yes, and your mom did too."

S: "O.K."

T: "Let's pretend it is before school and you come in to tell me what happened."

S: (Walks over to the door and pretends to come in.) "Good morning."

T: "Good morning. How are you?"

S: "Fine. Guess what."

T: "What?"

S: "Last night I went to the store with my mom. I saw the doctor."

T: "What doctor?"

S: "You remember. He came to our class yesterday."

T: "Oh, you saw that doctor."

S: "Yes. He talked to me and my mom."

T: "Well, how nice."

In this case the student finally was able to share the appropriate information with the teacher but only with questioning. The conversationally appropriate statement for the child to make would have been, "Last night I went to the store and I saw the doctor who came to our class." Procedures for having the child acquire this skill will be discussed within the Planning/Instruction Model.

Each of the preceding conversations was set up using familiar situations that are easily understood by the children. Additionally, a natural and logical dialogue brought about a need to use the objective chosen by the teacher. The objectives covered a variety of conversational skills, i.e., requesting using appropriate conjoining, commenting using a more appropriate sentence form and developing more complete extended turns. Thus, it can be seen that all aspects of conversation can be improved by carefully planned Conversational Scenarios.

It is also important to note that each scenario provided opportunities for children to practice appropriate use of the Structure (initiation, turn-taking and ending), Function (topic introduction and maintenance) and Form (syntax and morphology) of conversational discourse. This continual practice is crucial if hearing-impaired children are to achieve conversational competence.

Role-Playing

Teachers are often concerned about how to develop the ability to role-play in their students so that Conversational Scenarios can be utilized. The most critical element of successful role-playing is to create scenarios based on situations and characters with which the children are very familiar. In the examples given above, school and home are the contexts used. Scenarios need not be limited to these environments, but certainly for the young child, these are most productive.

Once the familiarity of context is established there are several strategies available to help children "get into" role-playing. Have the child watch as someone such as a teacher aide or an older child role-plays with the teacher. After the child watches a scenario being acted out s/he can act out the same one with the teacher. This strategy can be repeated a number of times over several days until the child is comfortable with the task.

A helpful technique for young children is to make "character aprons." These aprons depict typical attire of each of the children in a class, their parents and the teacher. Putting on the aprons helps children of four or five establish for themselves that they are playing a role. Using props is also very helpful. When doing scenarios about events at home the teacher can use pots and pans to help children feel they are in the kitchen. Tools can be used for scenarios that take place in the garage. Some children are helped by using simple picture books done by the teacher which highlight the setting, characters and events of a scenario. These need not be elaborate and, like the aprons and props, will not be needed for long. Children love to role-play and very quickly pick up this ability.

Another helpful activity is having children act out familiar stories. Pretending to be one of the "Billy Goats Gruff" or "Goldilocks" helps children acquire the concept of role playing. For children who have difficulty with this task, showing them pictures of familiar activities and then having them act them out is useful. In other words, after showing the appropriate picture have children pretend to read a book, ride a bike or play ball without any props. Older children just learning about scenarios and role playing enjoy portraying one of their favorite t.v. or movie characters.

Teachers who understand the Conversational Framework and Conversational Scenarios and students who are able to role play are essential precursors to the Planning/Instruction Model which follows.

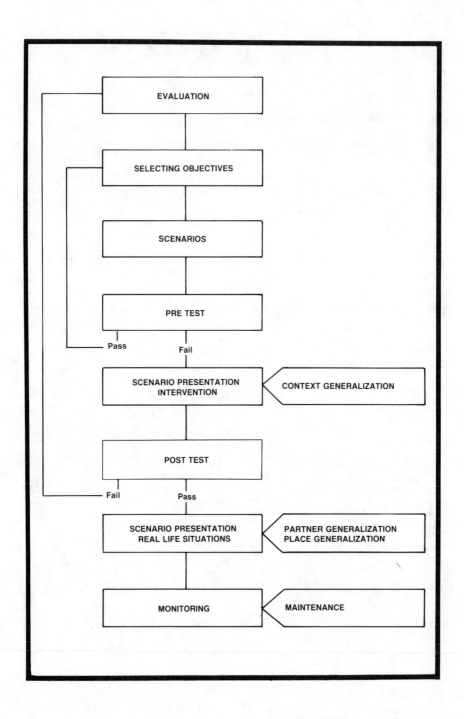

EVALUATION

SELECTING OBJECTIVES

SCENARIOS

PRE TEST

Pass · Fail

SCENARIO PRESENTATION INTERVENTION · CONTEXT GENERALIZATION

POST TEST

Fail · Pass

SCENARIO PRESENTATION REAL LIFE SITUATIONS · PARTNER GENERALIZATION PLACE GENERALIZATION

MONITORING · MAINTENANCE

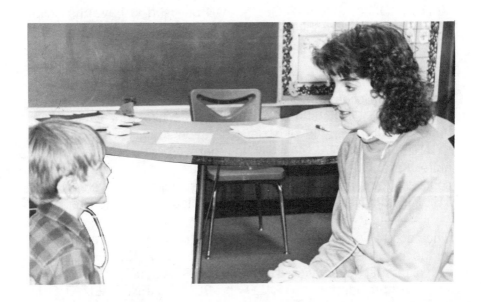

4 Planning/Instruction Model Overview

Effective instruction in all areas of the curriculum requires that teachers employ careful planning and systematic instructional procedures. This is certainly true for teachers who want their students to acquire mature conversational abilities. The model presented here is similar to those used by other writers. (Popham and Baker, 1970) It is made up of several steps which will be discussed briefly here and in detail later. A chart outlining the model appears opposite.

planning

(1) EVALUATION is the first step of instruction. Before teaching can begin it is necessary for the teacher to have a thorough understanding of each child's level of functioning. Ascertaining a child's conversational abilities requires examining his/her use of the Structure, Function and Form of discourse. Once evaluation is complete (2) the teacher is ready to begin SELECTING OBJECTIVES. These objectives will come from each of the areas of conversational dis-

course. The final step of planning comes with the design of CON-VERSATIONAL SCENARIOS that will be used to have the child achieve the desired objective.

Instruction begins with administering a PRE-TEST to the child to determine a baseline of performance against which the effectiveness of instruction can be reliably measured. Next is SCENARIO PRESENTATION and INTERVENTION. Effective work at this stage brings about the first level of generalization so critical for success, CONTEXT GENERALIZATION. In other words the student will acquire the ability to use the objective within a variety of linguistic contexts. To measure the child's acquisition of the objective a POST-TEST is administered which is similar or identical to the Pre-Test.

Once acquisition of the objective has been achieved it is necessary for the teacher to provide additional SCENARIO PRESENTATIONS with different conversational partners and REAL LIFE SITUATIONS which will provide for PARTNER and PLACE GENERALIZATION. These activities allow the student to learn to use his newly acquired skill with other people in different locations. The final and ongoing step of instruction is MONITORING of performance which tracks the MAINTENANCE of acquired learning by students.

At first glance utilizing this model of instruction appears somewhat cumbersome and time consuming. However, it is very manageable and efficient and even more importantly, it is effective and productive. Completing each of the steps in the model will maximize the effect of instruction and result in students who grow daily in their conversational abilities. The following pages present ideas and strategies to make this reality for every student and teacher.

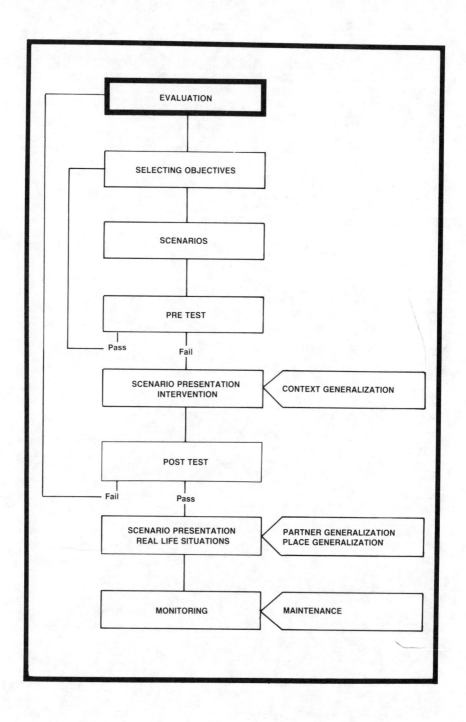

EVALUATION

SELECTING OBJECTIVES

SCENARIOS

PRE TEST

Pass   Fail

SCENARIO PRESENTATION
INTERVENTION   CONTEXT GENERALIZATION

POST TEST

Fail   Pass

SCENARIO PRESENTATION
REAL LIFE SITUATIONS   PARTNER GENERALIZATION
                               PLACE GENERALIZATION

MONITORING   MAINTENANCE

who does this? each teaches ? not Chris.

5 Evaluation

Effective instructional practice calls for two primary means of evaluation. One is the ongoing evaluation of instruction which occurs throughout the year. Strategies for this type of evaluation will be presented in later sections, i.e. Pre-Test, Post-Test and Monitoring. The second general means of evaluation is addressed here, i.e., evaluation used to establish a baseline of performance which is the beginning point of instruction for the year and which is also used to track growth on a year to year basis.

Three methods are available to teachers for evaluating the overall language performance of their students. The first procedure is to administer one or more standardized language tests. Several tests are widely used with normally hearing children. (See McLean and Snyder-McLean, 1978, for comments on several popular instruments.) There are two tests widely used with hearing-impaired children. The first of these, the Grammatial Analysis of Elicited Language, is actually a series of three tests: "GAEL—P Pre-Sentence Level" "GAEL—S Simple Sentence Level" and "GAEL—C Complex Sentence Level" (Moog and and Geers, 1979). These tests provide norms for hearing and hearing-impaired children and are made up of elicitation and imitation tasks which test for syntactic and morphologic abilities.

The other test widely used with hearing-impaired children is the "Test of Syntactic Abilities" (Quigley, et al, 1978) which as the title states measures the acquisition of specific syntactic constructions. It is a written test and normed only for children ten years and older. Both the GAEL series and the TSA provide useful information, but they are limited to narrow areas of conversational competence, i.e., syntax and morphology.

A second and more commonly used method of evaluation is for teachers to observe the language performance of children as they interact during the day and to determine omissions and errors. From these observations the teacher establishes the instructional objectives. However, this informal and unsystematic method does not result in an overall record of language proficiency. Consequently, objectives may be chosen which are developmentally inappropriate and valuable instructional time may be lost. It is therefore incumbent on teachers to use a more systematic means of evaluating performance. Procedures for accomplishing this are detailed in the following section.

The third method of evaluation is to carefully analyze a sample of the child's language. Several writers have described procedures for doing this. (Kretschmer and Kretschmer, 1978; Lee, 1974; and Miller, 1981). The procedures suggested by these authors have been modified somewhat for use with hearing-impaired children in classrooms. Specifically, the teacher creates and carries out a series of conversational scenarios and uses this data as the sample to be analyzed. While obtaining and analyzing a conversational sample requires more time than other approaches, it is the procedure of choice for teachers who want to be as certain as possible that they are utilizing their own and their student's time to the maximum.

Since the goal of instruction is to increase the student's conversational competence, it is necessary to obtain and analyze a variety of conversational samples from each child. The conversational scenarios used to accomplish this should be designed so that the teacher can evaluate each aspect of conversational discourse, i.e., Structure, Function and Form. The scenarios will include opportunities for determining how the child initiates, takes turns and ends conversation. They will provide information on how the child introduces and maintains topics using requests, comments, answers and acknowledgements. These scenarios will also provide the teacher information on how the child uses articles, pronouns and ellipsis to tie successive utterances together. They will also let the teacher know how well the child uses the extended turns of narrating, explaining, describing and giving directions. Finally the teacher will be able to determine the linguistic forms which the child uses productively and those forms which need to be developed.

Procedure

Obtaining a conversation sample is best accomplished by tape recording (audio or preferably, video) a series of conversational scenarios and then transcribing the dialogues. (Care should be taken in obtaining the sample so that the child's utterances are always audible.) The transcription should include both teacher and child utterances as well as any relevant gestures by either. A minimum of fifty child utterances from seven to ten scenarios is required to gain a broad picture of the child's ability. (Note: These transcriptions can also be used to complete a "Phonologic Level Speech Evaluation" as described by Ling, 1976). To ensure that the sample contains examples of all the major elements of conversation, the following guidelines are offered:

1. The scenarios should call for the student to initiate and end conversation with a variety of role play partners of different social status and age, e.g., parents, adults, children, etc.

2. The scenarios should call for the student to use comments and requests to introduce topics.

3. The scenarios should be carried out so that the student will need to request clarification.

4. The scenarios should contain opportunity for the student to use each of the extended turns.

5. The scenarios should contain opportunity for several single turn exchanges.

Evaluation Questions

Once the sample has been collected and transcribed, the teacher can begin evaluating the sample. This is done by answering the questions listed below on the "Conversational Competence Evaluation Form" which appears on pages 44 through 50.

Structure

1. Does the child have a repertoire of initiating routines?
2. Are the initiating routines used appropriate to the age and status of the partner?
3. Does the child wait until his conversational partner stops speaking before beginning his turn?
4. Are the child's utterances consistently contingent upon the prior utterances?
5. Does the child end conversation with a variety of routines?
6. Are the ending routines used appropriate to the age and status of the conversational partner?

Function

7. Does the child provide sufficient information for the conversation partner when introducing topics?
8. Does the child use comments and requests to introduce topics?
9. Does the child maintain topics?
10. Does the child use comments, requests, answers and acknowledgements to maintain topics?
11. Does the child request clarification?
12. Are requests for clarification specific?
13. Does the child use the topic cohension devices of articles, pronouns and ellipsis?
14. When providing a narrative does the child:
    a. Use an opening statement that includes all elements of the setting?
    b. Present an initiating event which includes the problem or goal?
    c. List the action(s) taken in appropriate sequence?

d. Include an appropriate ending?

e. Use a variety of connectors to indicate time and causal relationships?

15. When giving directions does the child:
    a. Use a beginning point which is clear to the listener?
    b. Sequence the actions correctly?
    c. Use locative terms including prepositional phrases and directions?
    d. Include appropriate time connectors to sequence actions:

16. When giving an explanation does the child:
    a. Begin with an organizing statement which clearly defines the outcome?
    b. Identify the materials to be used?
    c. Sequence correctly the actions to be taken?
    d. Use a variety of time connectors?
    e. Use a variety of appropriate verbs?

17. When giving a description does the child:
    a. Include only the distinctive features of the object or person?
    b. Use relative clauses and "with" phrases?
    c. Use a variety of descriptive terms?

Form

18. For the child at the one to three-word utterance level which semantic categories and/or semantic relationships are present?
    For the child producing three-word utterances and longer what levels of syntactic and morphologic usage are present?

Suggested Sequence

The following sequence has been found to be effective in completing the Evaluation Form:

1. Read through one complete scenario.
2. List examples of correct and incorrect usage of semantic and/or syntactic items on the FORM section of the evalu-

ation using parentheses to indicate missing elements and incorrect usage. (See pages 65 and 66)

3. Repeat steps one and two for each of the scenarios.

4. Reread each scenario and assess the quality of the extended turns, noting strengths and weaknesses on the evaluation form. (See pages 64 and 65)

5. Check each scenario for quality of topic introduction, maintenance and cohesion, noting such on the evaluation form. (See pages 62 and 63)

6. Check each scenario for quality and appropriateness of initiating, turn-taking and ending. (See pages 62 and 63)

7. Add pertinent information to each section of the evaluation based on knowledge of the child's conversational abilities not reflected within the sample. These should be marked with an asterisk.

8. Summarize the evaluation by listing the child's strengths and weaknesses, and questions which need to be answered to make the evaluation complete. (See pages 67 and 68)

This evaluation will serve as a permanent record of the child's performance and as the basis for selecting the initial teaching objectives for the year. As time progresses the teacher will identify additional areas of concern that will require instruction. Evaluation is an ongoing process and the teacher needs to be alert to the strengths and weaknesses of each child's conversation on a continual basis.

CONVERSATIONAL COMPETENCE EVALUATION
Tucker-Maxon Oral School

Name _____ **Age** _____ **Date** _____

Evaluator _____

STRUCTURE

Initiation _____

_____

Turn-Taking _____

_____

Ending _____

_____

FUNCTION

Topic Introduction

Comments _____

_____

Requests _____

_____

Topic Maintenance

Comments _____

_____

Requests _____

_____

Answers _____

_____

Acknowledgements _____

_____

Requests Clarification _____

_____

Topical Cohesion

Articles _____

Pronouns _____

Ellipsis _____

Extended Turns

Narratives _____

_____

_____

_____

_____

_____

_____

Directions _____

_____

_____

_____

_____

_____

Explanation _____

_____

_____

_____

_____

_____

Description _____

_____

_____

_____

_____

_____

FORM

One-Word Semantic Categories _____

_____

_____

Two-Word Semantic Relationships _____

_____

_____

_____

Three-Word Semantic Relationships _____

_____

_____

Noun Phrase _____

_____

Verb Phrase _____

_____

Negation _____

_____

Yes/No Questions _____

_____

WH-Questions _____

_____

Conjoining _____

_____

Relative Clauses _____

_____

Adverbial Clauses _____

_____

Noun Clauses _____

_____

Infinitives _____

_____

Participles _____

SUMMARY

Structure

Strengths _____

_____

_____

Weaknesses _____

_____

_____

Questions _____

_____

_____

Function

Strengths _____

_____

_____

_____

Weaknesses _____

_____

_____

_____

Questions _____

_____

_____

_____

Form

Strengths _____

_____

_____

Weaknesses _____

_____

_____

Questions _____

_____

_____

Sample Evaluation

The following pages present a conversational sample obtained by using a series of scenarios with a nine-year-old profoundly hearing-impaired girl. These scenarios were designed according to the guidelines listed on pages 41 to 44. Immediately following each scenario are comments on the conversational strengths and weaknesses present. (The teacher is identified as T and the child utterances are coded C1, C2, C3, etc. to facilitate reference to the comments.) The Scenarios and comments are followed by a completed _Conversational Competence Evaluation_ based on the sample.

Scenario One—Narrative	Comments on Scenario One—Narrative
T: "Let's pretend that I am your friend and you come home from camping. One night while you were sleeping a bear came and knocked over some garbage cans. Everybody was scared."	
C1 "O.K."	**C1** Acknowledged understanding of scenario.
T: "I'll be here playing and you come outside and tell me about your camping trip."	
C2 "O.K." (Child crosses room and then pretends to be coming outside and sees her friend.)	**C2** Acknowledged understanding.
C3 "Hi."	**C3** Initiated conversation appropriately.
T: "Hi. Did you have fun on your camping trip?"	
C4 "Yes, I saw the bear. The bear said, "Grrr." I sleeping. And then I hear. Everybody sleeping and couldn't hear. Then I saw big bear. And then, and then, "Grrr." Then bear eat garbage food."	**C4** Answered request for information. Produced poorly formed narrative. No setting statement. Sequence of actions is unclear, but does attempt use of time connectors. Resolution of problem is not present. Inappropriate use of "the" to introduce bear. Inconsistent use of verb tense. Left out auxiliary verbs. Conjoined using "and." Used negative contraction. Used direct discourse.

Scenario One—Narrative (con't.)	Comments on Scenario One—Narrative
T: (Pause to allow time for child to elaborate) "Wow. Were you scared?"	
C5 "Yes. I thought bear eat me."	**C5** Answered request for information. Attempted to use noun clause complement, but left out verb auxiliary.
T: "Boy that was really exciting for everybody."	
C6 "Yeah."	**C6** Acknowledged comment.
T: "Well, I have to go now. See you later."	
C7 "O.K. See you later."	**C7** Ended conversation appropriately.

Scenario Two—Narrative	Comments on Scenario Two—Narrative
T: "This time I'll be your teacher and you come to school with a cast on your leg. You were riding your bike and a cat ran in front of you. You turned very fast and fell down and broke your leg."	
C1 "O.K." (Goes to the door and pretends to come into the room limping.)	**C1** Acknowledged understanding of scenario.
T: "Oh my goodness, what happened to you?"	
C2 "Well, I fell off the bike."	**C2** Answered request for information. Used well-formed sentence. Used "the" instead of pronoun "my."
T: "Oh, I'm sorry."	
C3 "I saw a kitty. I couldn't stop. And then I turn very quickly. I fell down. I broke my leg. I can't play. The doctor said, 'For six weeks.'"	**C3** Produced incomplete narrative. No setting statement. Good problem statement and conclusion. Inconsistent use of time connectors. Used simple sentences consistently with good verb tense. Used pronouns. Used negative contraction. Used adverb. Used direct discourse.
T: "Oh dear. Did you hurt anything else?"	
C4 "Just my leg, not arm."	**C4** Answered request for information.
T: "Oh good."	
C5 "Yeah."	**C5** Acknowledged comment.
T: "Well, it's almost time for school. Will you please get ready."	
C6 "O.K."	**C6** Acknowledged request for action.

Scenario Three—Directions	Comments on Scenario Three—Directions
T: "This time you will be working in the office. I'll be a delivery person with some books for the library. I'll come in and ask you how to get there. O.K.?"	
C1 "I work in office?"	**C1** Requested clarification. *omitted article*
T: "Yes. You are the secretary."	
C2 "O.K."	**C2** Acknowledged comment.
T: "Let's start. You sit there and I'll come to the office." (As delivery person) "Pardon me. Can you tell me where the library is. I have these books."	
C3 "Yes. Upstairs over there. (Points) Big school over there."	**C3** Answered request for information. Provided poorly formed directions. No point of origin. No sequence of actions. Incomplete information. Included two locative terms.
T: "O.K. Thank you."	
C4 "You're welcome."	**C4** Used appropriate ending.

Scenario Four—Explanation	Comments on Scenario Four—Explanation
T: "This time I'll be your friend Heather. You bring some cake to school in your lunch. You let me have a piece. I'll ask you how you made it because it tastes so good."	
C1 "O.K."	**C1** Acknowledged understanding of scenario.
T: "Let's pretend we're in the lunch room."	
C2 "O.K."	**C2** Acknowledged understanding of location.
T: "Let's start."	
C3 "Hi, Heather."	**C3** Initiated conversation appropriately.
T: (As Heather) "Hi."	
C4 "You want some cake?"	**C4** Requested information. Omitted auxiliary.
T: "Yes, please."	
C5 (Pretends to hand piece of cake to Heather.) "Here."	**C5** Accompanied physical action with verbal comment.
T: "Thank you." (Pretends to eat.) "Umm, that's good. Did you make it?"	
C6 "Yes."	**C6** Answered request for information.
T: "How did you do it?"	

Scenario Four—Explanation (con't.)	Comments on Scenario Four—Explanation
C7 First, chocolate cake, not frosting. You put sugar, milk, egg. And the frosting; sugar, some milk, flour, eggs. That's it."	**C7** Answered request for information. Provided inadequate explanation. Unclear directions. Two time connectors. Used only one verb.
T: (Pause) "Oh, I see."	
C8 "Then I put oven five minutes. And then I went to bed. In morning I bring cake. You like cake?"	**C8** Used three time connectors. Used inconsistent verb tense. Requested information. Omitted auxiliary in question. Used noun (cake) instead of pronoun.
T: "Very much."	
C9 "If you like cake you want give your mom?"	**C9** Requested information. Used conditional adverbial clause. Used noun instead of pronoun. Omitted auxiliary in question clause.
T: "Yes that would be very nice. Thank you."	
C10 "You're welcome."	**C10** Ended appropriately.

Scenario Five—Description	Comments on Scenario Five—Description
T: "Let's pretend that I am your mom. You come home from the mall. You saw a beautiful dress and you want to have it. When you get home you tell me all about it."	
C1 "O.K."	**C1** Acknowledged understanding of scenario.
T: "Are you ready?"	
C2 "Yes."	**C2** Answered request for information.
T: "All right. I'll be at home and you come in."	
C3 (Goes to door and pretends to come in.) "Hi Mom."	**C3** Initiated appropriately.
T: (As Mom) "Hi. Did you have fun at the mall?"	
C4 "I look for clothes for special day."	**C4** Answered request for information. Used incorrect verb tense.
T: "Did you find something?"	
C5 "I found dress. Blue over there. (Points) Ribbon over there. (Points) Bow over there. (Points) It on my tummy right there. (Points) And short sleeve and long white. You wanna buy?"	**C5** Answered request for information. Provided inadequate description. Distinctive features are present. Needed additional vocabulary. Requested information. Omitted auxiliary and pronoun.
T: "Umm. It sounds pretty."	
C6 "Can I buy? I know how much money."	**C6** Requested information Included auxiliary. Omitted final pronoun. Commented. Used inappropriate form.
T: "Well, we'll see.	
C7 "Please."	**C7** Requested action. Used ellipsis.
T: "Let's talk to your dad."	
C8 "O.K."	**C8** Acknowledged comment.

Scenario Six—Description	Comments on Scenario Six—Description
T: "This time let's pretend that you are walking to school and you see someone stealing a bike. So you call the police and tell them what happened. I'll be the policeman."	
C1 "O.K."	**C1** Acknowledged understanding of scenario.
T: "Let's start."	
C2 (Pretending to walk to school.) Says to herself, "Oh no! Steal the bike. (Pretends to find phone booth and make a call.)	**C2** Commented on action. Inappropriate verb tense.
T: "Hello. Police Department."	
C3 "This is D. I need help. The boy stole the bike."	**C3** Initiated appropriately. Twice used "the" to introduce new information.
T: "What did it look like?"	
C4 "It blue, a blue seat and brake."	**C4** Answered request for information. Provided almost adequate description. Included distinctive features. Omitted "with". Omitted verb.
T: "What did the boy look like?"	
C5 "A blue jacket and brown hair with blue eyes and red stripe shirt and brown pants. That's it."	**C5** Answered request for information. Provided unorganized description. Used "with" phrase. Alternated clothing and physical features. Conjoined using "and."
T: "Thank you for calling. We will try to find the boy and the bike."	
C6 "You're welcome."	**C6** Ended appropriately.

Scenario Seven— Conversation	Comments on Scenario Seven— Conversation
T: "Now I will pretend to be your mom and you be yourself. You go over to your friend Rachel's house and she has some new puppies. You would like to have one. So you come home and ask your mom if you can have one. O.K.?"	
C1: "O.K." (Walks to door and pretends to come in)."Mom."	**C1** Acknowledged understanding of scenario. Initiated appropriately.
T: (As mom) "What?"	
C2: "I saw Rachel have puppy. Rachel have four puppy. Can I take one?"	**C2** Commented. Attempted to conjoin but omitted connector. Used incorrect form of verb. Commented. Used incorrect form of verb. Omitted plural marker. Requested information. Included auxiliary.
T: "Will you take care of it?"	
C3: "I take care of puppy."	**C3** Answered request for information. Omitted Tense marker. Used noun instead of pronoun.
T: "Mmmm."	
C4 "Feed the dog and make for a doghouse.	**C4** Expanded answer to request for information. Omitted subject. Omitted tense marker. Confused verb phrase.
T: "Well, I don't know."	
C5 "I feed him dog food. Brush hair and put bow on."	**C5** Acknowledged comment. Omitted tense marker. Omitted subject.
T: "O.K. You can."	
C6 "Oh, thank you. I will call Rachel."	**C6** Acknowledged comment. Commented. Included tense marker.

Scenario Eight—Conversation	Comments on Scenario Eight—Conversation
T: "Let's pretend that I am your mom and you are yourself. Your friend Jody calls and wants you to go to a movie. You ask me about it. I will be Jody, too."	
C1 "O.K."	**C1** Acknowledged understanding of scenario.
T: (As Jody, pretends to call.) "Ring. Ring."	
C2 "Hello."	**C2** Initiated appropriately.
T: "Hi, this is Jody."	
C3 "What you want?"	**C3** Responded inappropriately to initiation of partner. Requested information Omitted auxiliary.
T: "Can you go to a movie with me tonight?"	
C4 "Oh, I ask mommy."	**C4** Answered request for information. Omitted tense marker.
C5 (To mom) "Mom, can I go to movie with Jody?"	**C5** Requested information. Included auxiliary. Omitted article.
T: (As mom) "When?"	

Scenario Eight—Conversation (con't.)	Comments on Scenario Eight—Conversation
C6 "I ask Jody when."	**C6** Answered request for information. Omitted auxiliary. Used noun clause complement.
C7 (To Jody) "Jody, when we go to movie?"	**C7** Requested information. Omitted auxiliary.
T: (As Jody) "Tonight."	
C8 "Mom, tonight."	**C8** Completed answering request for information.
T: "Oh, I'm sorry. Your cousins are coming over to play."	
C9 "I tell Jody."	**C9** Comment. Omitted auxiliary.
C10 (To Jody) "I'm sorry I can't go because I have play my cousin. I can go maybe next time."	**C10** Completed answering request for information. Used noun clause complement. Used negative contraction. Used causal connector. Attempted to use infinitive but omitted "to". Commented. Placed conditional word inappropriately.
T: "O.K."	
C11 "Bye."	**C11** Ended appropriately.

The following pages present a completed *Conversational Competence Evaluation* based on this sample. This evaluation reflects the comments made on the preceding pages concerning this student's conversational ability. (Additional samples of scenario transcripts, comments and evaluations appear as Appendix A.) Once the evaluation is complete the teacher is ready to select appropriate teaching objectives. This important step is addressed beginning on Page 70.

CONVERSATIONAL COMPETENCE EVALUATION
Tucker-Maxon Oral School

Name D.L.   **Age** 9 **Date** 5/8/88

Evaluator Staff

STRUCTURE

Initiation   "Hi". "Hi Heather". "Mom". "This is D". "Hello."

Turn-Taking   Consistently contingent.

Ending   "See you later". "You're welcome". "Good-Bye."

FUNCTION

Topic Introduction

Comments   "This is D". "I need help". "I saw R". "have puppy."

Requests   "You want some cake?"

Topic Maintenance

Comments   "I know how much money". "I found dress". "Feed the dog" ... "I will call Rachel."

Requests   "If you like" ... "you want give ...?" "You like cake?" "Can I go?" "You wanna buy?" "Can I take one?" "What you want?" "When ...?"

Answers   "Did you ...?" "Were you ...?" "What happened ...?" "Are you ready?" "What did it look like?" "Can you ...?"

Acknowledgements   "O.K." "Yeah"

Requests Clarification   I work in office?

Topical Cohesion

Articles ‘the’ to introduce topic

Pronouns ‘the’ instead of ‘my’. Used I/You/We/Me—Missed

several/it/opportunities

Ellipsis

Extended Turns

Narratives Incomplete

No setting statement

Inconsistent inclusion of problem/resolution

Inconsistent use of time connectors.

Uses simple sentences inconsistently.

Verb tense is inconsistent.

Directions Poorly formed.

No point of origin.

No sequence of actions

Included two locative terms.

Explanation Inadequate

Unclear statements and sequence

Included two time connectors _____

Used only one verb. _____

_____

_____

_____

Description __Not adequate_____

Included distinctive features _____

Lexicon inadequate _____

No use of 'with' phrase _____

_____

_____

_____

FORM

One-Word Semantic Categories _____

_____

_____

Two-Word Semantic Relationships _____

_____

_____

_____

Three-Word Semantic Relationships _____

_____

Noun Phrase big bear/big school/special day/red stripe shirt/

four puppy/

___

Verb Phrase saw/said, ' '/ (was) sleeping/hear (heard)/will

call/eat (ate)/fell off/turn very quickly/put (in)/take care

of/looked for/steal(ing) the bike/It (is) blue/... make for

.../I'm

Negation couldn't/can't/not (my) arm/

___

Yes/No Questions (Do) you want ...?/(Do) you like ...?/(do)

you want give? (Do) you want buy? Can I buy? Can I go ...?

WH-Questions When we go ...? What (do) you want?

___

Conjoining ... and .../And then .../

___

Relative Clauses

___

Adverbial Clauses If you .../... because ...

___

Noun Clauses I thought bear eat me./I know how much .../

I'm sorry I can't go .../I ask Jody when./

Infinitives have (to) play/

___

why add info in parentheses?

Participles _____

SUMMARY

Structure

Strengths _Good initiation, turn-taking & ending._

_____

_____

Weaknesses _____

_____

_____

Questions _____

_____

_____

Function

Strengths _Introduces and maintains topics well. Uses all_

intents. Answers wide variety of questions.

_____

Weaknesses _Narratives—setting and time connectors. Direc-_

tions need origin statement and lexicon. Explanations need

sentences. Need consistent pronouns and articles.

Questions _____

_____

_____

Form

Strengths <u>Simple sentences predominate. Attempts</u>

<u>conjoining, adverbial clauses, noun clauses and infinitives</u>

Weaknesses <u>Verb tense inconsistent. Lack of auxiliary in</u>

<u>question forms.</u>

_____

Questions <u>Relative clauses</u>

_____

_____

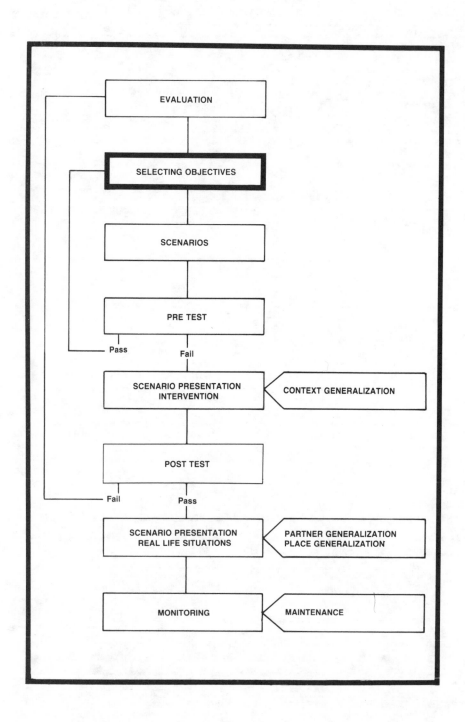

EVALUATION

SELECTING OBJECTIVES

SCENARIOS

PRE TEST

Pass   Fail

SCENARIO PRESENTATION
INTERVENTION   CONTEXT GENERALIZATION

POST TEST

Fail   Pass

SCENARIO PRESENTATION
REAL LIFE SITUATIONS   PARTNER GENERALIZATION
PLACE GENERALIZATION

MONITORING   MAINTENANCE

6 Selecting Objectives

Choosing appropriate instructional objectives is perhaps the most important task facing teachers of hearing-impaired children. Each student has a limited amount of time to acquire the vast array of skills and knowledge necessary to become a competent conversational partner. The instructional objectives chosen by the teacher will directly influence the child for a lifetime. This dictates that the teacher follow a systematic plan which brings about the orderly acquisition of conversational skills.

The *Stages of Conversational Development* presented on Pages 73 through 81 is such a systematic plan. It is comprised of four stages which reflect the normal development of conversation. Each stage is made up of objectives which address the structure and function of conversation including the development of the extended turns. At the conclusion of each stage the linguistic forms which will be learned to express the objectives are listed.

Conversational Skill Objectives

Linguistic form is best learned when it serves the Structure and Function of conversation. Normally developing children learn correct linguistic form because it achieves conversational purposes. When hearing-impaired children are learning within a conversational model they have the opportunity to learn in a similar manner. That is, linguistic form is learned to express conversational purposes. Learning which has a clear purpose is preferable to that which has no conceived purpose. For this reason each of the *Stages of Conversational Development* focuses on the Structure and Function of conversation and presents the linguistic forms to be learned, not as objectives, but as the means to express those objectives.

To reflect this important concept, instructional objectives will be of two types. The first type will address a specific conversational skill without reference to a linguistic form. For example:

- The student will maintain topics by commenting following a comment. (Stage One)
- The student will produce a setting statement within a narrative which includes all the important characters. (Stage Two)
- The student will initiate conversations with visitors to the classroom using known routines. (Stage Three)

- the student will request clarification by asking for specific information. (Stage Four)

The second type of objective also will address a conversational skill and will include reference to a specific linguistic form which will express that skill. For example:

- The student will introduce conversational topics using Agent and Action statements. (Stage One)
- The student will request information using "who," "what" and "where" questions. (Stage Two)
- The student will produce an explanation which includes a conditional clause introduced by "if". (Stage Three)
- The student will produce a narrative which includes use of "while" and "since" to express time relationships.

By writing objectives which always specify a conversational skill the teacher is planning instruction in a manner that focuses on the most important elements of conversation to be attained. Choosing the most appropriate objectives is facilitated by the *Stages of Conversational Development*. By comparing the completed *Conversational Competence Evaluation Form* with information contained in the Stages the teacher can determine which skills the child should acquire next.

Stages of Conversational Development

Stage One establishes the basic conversational set. Children learn to initiate conversations, respond to initiations and take turns within conversation. Following this they learn to introduce and maintain topics by commenting, requesting, answering and acknowledging. These conversational turns are expressed using one-, two- and three-word utterances. Instruction will make provision for the child to acquire each of these semantic categories and semantic relationships to serve the conversational objectives.

Stage Two adds additional initiation routines and calls for their use with a wider variety of persons. Three-word utterances are used to request information and beginning clarification requests are introduced. Basic skill with extended turns is acquired along with beginning use of pronouns and articles. The aspects of linguistic form to be incorporated include early forms of negation; conjoining with "and"; simple relative clauses and infinitives; and some aspects of noun and verb phrases.

Stage Three expands initiation by introducing idiomatic expressions and increasing the number of persons engaged in conversation. Requests for information are expanded and refined and requests for clarification become more specific. The extended turns become longer, more complete and cohesive. Earlier acquired linguistic forms are refined and expanded and adverbial clauses and noun clauses are introduced.

Stage Four is the final step in acquisition of conversational competence. Requests for information are expanded and requests for clarification become very specific. The extended turns become complete and additional complex linguistic forms are added.

The following pages present the Stages of Conversational Development.

STAGE ONE	
Student action:	**Examples:**
1. Spontaneously initiate conversations with others and respond to the initiations of others.	**1.** S: "Hi." T: "Hi." T: "Johnny." S: "What?"
2. Take turns within conversation.	**2.** T: "Hi." S: "Hi." T: "How are you?" S: "Fine. How are you?" T: "Fine."
3.(a) Spontaneously introduce topices by commenting. **(b)** Spontaneously introduce topics by requesting.	**3.(a)** "I go store." "Look. New shoes." **(b)** "Play outside?" "Where mommy?"
4.(a) Maintain topics by acknowledging.	**4.(a)** T: "That's pretty." S: "Thank you." T: "Look at that big tree." S: "Yeah."
(b) Maintain topics by answering.	**(b)** T: "Where is your lunch box?" S: "There." T: "Do you have your money?" S: "Yes."
(c) Maintain topics by commenting.	**(c)** T: "I have a new puppy at home." S: "I have puppy." T: "I like apple juice." S: "I not like."
(d) Maintain topics by requesting.	**(d)** T: "Johnny is not here today." S: "Johnny sick?" T: "Mary hurt her knee." S: "What happened?

The following semantic relationships will be developed to express the above-listed conversational skills on page 74:

Existence—"That one."
Recurrence—"More juice."
Non Existence—"No ball.
   "Allgone milk."
Denial—"No do."
Rejection—"No car."
Agent and Action—"Mommy go."
Action and Object—"Push car."
Agent and Object—"Daddy car."
Action and Location—"Go store."
Entity and Location—"Ball here."
Attribute and Entity—"Big boy."
Experiencer and Process—"You
   think." "I like."

Process and Entity—"Want ball."
Action and Recipient—"Give
   mommy."
Action and Instrument—"Sweep
   broom."
Agent and Action and Object—
   "Daddy hit ball."
Agent and Action and Location—
   "I go store."
Action and Object and
   Location—"Put cookie there."
Experiencer and Process and
   Object—"I want milk."

STAGE TWO	
Student action:	**Examples:**
1. Initiate conversations with a wide variety of other persons using the routines acquired in Stage One.	
Initiate conversations using various expressions.	"Good morning." "Hello, Mary."
2. Take multiple turns around topics introduced by self and others.	
3.(a) Request information by using three-word utterances with rising intonation.	"Mommy go store?" "I play outside?"
(b) Request information by using WH-questions.	"What Johnny doing?" "Where Johnny going?" "Who is that?"
4. Request clarification at appropriate times during conversation.	"What?" "Pardon me."

STAGE TWO—cont'd

Student action:	Examples:
5. Produce narratives within conversation which include the primary characters and a series of actions.	"Me and Mommy go to store. Mommy drive car. Buy cookies and milk. Go home."
6. Produce explanations within conversations which are made up of a series of actions.	"Pour in milk. Put powder in. Stir up. Put in refrigerator."
7. Produce simple directions using a variety of locative terms.	"Go over there." "Go down stairs."
8. Produce descriptions which include only distinctive features using a variety of adjectives.	"I want blue ball." (As opposed to the red one.) "See my new shoes." (As opposed to the old ones.)
9. Use pronouns (I, she, he, we, they, it) to indicate old information. Use "the" to signal old information and "a" to signal new information.	

The following syntactic constructions and morphologic markers will be used to express the conversational skills listed above:

- Negation
  "no" "not" "can't" "don't"
- Conjoining
  "and" to join words and successive clauses.
- Relative Clause
  Attach a specifier clause to an indefinite form.
  "The thing I bought." "The one you have."
- Infinitive
  Used with "have" and "want".
  "I want to see." "I have to go."

- Verb Phrase
  Present progressive with some verbs.
  Regular and irregular past used inconsistently.
  Copula verbs—"was" and "am".
  Auxiliaries—"will" "can"
- Noun Phrase
  Possessive pronouns—"my" "mine" "your(s)".
  Demonstrative pronouns—"this" "that".
  Possessive nouns using "-'s".

STAGE THREE

Student action:	Examples:
1. Initiate conversations using idiomatic expressions.	"How's it goin' " "Guess what?"
Initiate conversations with new persons using appropriate routines.	
2. Carry on extended conversations of multiple turns with teacher and/or peers utilizing all of the conversational intents.	
3. Request information using yes/no questions with the auxiliary inverted.	"Am I going?" "Can I have it?" "Do you like it?"
Request information using WH-questions.	"Where is Johnny going?" "What is Johnny doing?" "Why are you here?" "How you do that?" "What for?" "How come?" "When are we going?" "Why not?"
4. Request clarification using more polite forms.	"What did you say?" "Pardon me." "I didn't hear you."
5. Produce narratives which include all elements of the setting, a problem or goal statement, one or more episodes and a resolution. Some time and causal connectors are present.	"Last Saturday my family went to the beach. We wanted to see whales. We watched for a long time but didn't see any. Then we ate our lunch and came home."
6. Produce explanations which include an organizing statement, materials and sequence of actions. Some time and causal connectors are present.	"I will show you how. First, everybody has seven cards. I ask for card that I have. You give me the card. If you don't have card then you say "Go fish."

STAGE THREE—cont'd

Student action:	Examples:
7. Produce directions which have a clear point of origin and use a variety of locative terms.	"Go down the hall to the blue door. Go outside. Walk across the playground and then go in the red door. Turn right. There is the gym.
8. Produce descriptions which include all distinctive features and use "with phrases" and a variety of descriptive terms.	"I got a new dress. It is red with white stripes. It has long sleeves and big white buttons. And it has a big collar.
9. Expand use of pronouns to indicate old information. Expand use of articles to signal old and new information.	

STAGE THREE

- **The following syntactic constructions and morphologic markers will be used to express the conversational skills listed above.**

- Negation
    Expressed by "won't"
    "doesn't" "isn't" "aren't"
    "didn't" "couldn't" and "never"

- Conjoining
    Words and successive
    clauses joined using "but"
    and "or".

- Relative Clause
    Attach a specifier clause to
    the object of the main clause.
    "I got the book that you
    wanted."

- Adverbial Clause
    Time relationships
    expressed by "when" "before"
    and "after".
        "When my brother comes
        we are going to play."
        "After school I am going
        downtown."

    Causal relationships expressed
    by "because" and "so".
        "She put on her coat
        because it was cold."
        "The ball was flat so he
        pumped it up."

    Conditional relationships
    expressed by "if".
        "If you want more candy
        ask Mom."

STAGE THREE
syntactic constructions and morphologic markers cont'd

Student action:	Examples:

• Infinitive
  Used with various process
  verbs.
  "I want to buy a new coat."
  "I like to ski."
 	
• Noun Clause
  Introduced by "that" "where"
  "what" and "who".
  　"I wish that I could go."
  　"Dad doesn't know where
  　it is."
  　"She heard what he said."
  　"Johnny remembered who
  　won the prize."
	• Verb Phrase
	  Regular past forms used
	  consistently.
	  Past progressive.
	  Copula—"is" "are" "was"
	  "were" and contracted forms.
	  Auxiliaries—"am going" to
	  indicate future as in "I am
	  going to the ball game
	  tomorrow."
	
	• Noun Phrase
	  Possessive pronouns—"his"
	  "her"
	  Demonstrative pronouns—
	  "these" "those"
	  Comparative and superlative
	  adjectives—"bigger"
	  "biggest"

STAGE FOUR

Student action:	Examples:
1. Initiate conversations using routines appropriate to the age and status of the intended partner.	
2. Introduce topics that are of high interest to the conversational partner.	
3.(a) Request information using yes/no tag questions.	"They finished their work, didn't they?" "They didn't finish their work, did they?"
(b) Request information using WH-questions	"Which one of them did it?" "What if we go?" "Where did you go?" "What do you want to do?"

STAGE FOUR—cont'd

Student action:	Examples:
4. Request clarification using specific requests.	"Where did you go?" "What time did you say?"
5. Produce narratives that are complete using extensive time and causal connectors.	"During August my brother and I are going to Boy Scout Camp for three days. I'm so excited because I can earn more merit badges. When we get there we have to find a place for our tent. Then we put it up and ask the Scoutmaster to check it out. After that we have free time until lunch. After lunch we can choose what badges to work on. Then we work on them for three days and have fun, too. We can swim and ride horses and go on hikes. It's really going to be fun."
6. Produce complete explanations for activities that are removed from school, in which no props are present and that incorporate extensive connectors and a variety of verbs.	"Well, it's really easy to do. First, decide how much ground you have and what you want to plant. Then, dig up the ground you want to use and make it very soft. After that rake up all the rocks. When you're finished smooth it out. Now you are ready to plant your seeds."
7. Produce a complete set of directions for a destination far removed from the beginning point which incorporate a variety of locative terms and connectors.	"It's easy to get to my house from school. Go up Holgate to 92nd. Turn left and go to the first stoplight which is Powell Boulevard. Go right on Powell and look for the sign for I-205. Go on 205 across the bridge and take the third exit."
8. Produce clear descriptions which relate two or more dimensions incorporating a variety of descriptive terms.	"Well, he is about six feet tall with dark brown hair and blue eyes. He was wearing a blue sport coat and gray flannel slacks with a white shirt and striped tie. He drove away in a little blue sports car."

The following syntactic constructions and morphologic markers will be used to express the conversational skills listed on page 80.

- Conjoining
  Words and clauses joined by using "either-or" and "neither-nor".

- Relative Clause
  Embed a specifier clause after the subject of the main clause, with the WH word replacing the subject of the embedded clause. "The boy that is playing is my bother."
  Attach a specifier clause to the object of the main sentence with the WH word replacing the subject of the attached clause. "She petted the dog that is barking."

- Adverbial Clause
  Time relationships expressed using "while" and "since".
  "While everyone is singing I will make the punch.
  "She has been waiting since four o'clock this afternoon."

Causal relationships expressed using "therefore".
"You are late turning in this report, therefore you will not get credit for it."

Conditional relationships expressed using "unless".
"We can not leave unless you are on time."

- Infinitive
  Used following an adjective. "They were smart to leave."

  Used when the subjects in each clause are different. "I want you to go home."

  Used as the subject. "To win this race you must start out fast."

- Noun Clause
  Use of WH-infinitive clause. "I know how to do it."

Comparing the information contained in the *Stages of Conversational Development* with the results of the *Conversational Competence Evaluation* will allow the teacher to determine the most important instructional objectives for each child. By carefully examining student performance in comparison with each stage of development, the teacher can write objectives and plan instruction which take into account child need, stage of development and time constraints faced by both teacher and student.

Sample Set of Objectives

Listed below are ten of the weaknesses determined to be present in the conversational ability of the student evaluated in the previous section. Accompanying these weaknesses are the instructional objectives which when attained will do the most to enhance her conversational ability. They are listed in order of importance as determined by the *Stages of Conversational Development*.

Student Weaknesses	Objectives
1. Incomplete setting statement in narratives.	1. Within conversation the student will provide a complete setting when giving a narrative.
2. Lack of a clear point of origin in directions.	2. Within conversation the student will establish a clear point of origin when giving directions.
3. Inconsistent use of simple sentences in explanations.	3. Within conversation the student will use complete sentences when giving an explanation.
4. Limited use of pronouns to signal old information.	4. Within conversation the child will use "he", "she" and "it" to signal old information.
5. Use of "the" to signal new information.	5. Within conversation the student will use "a" to signal new information.
6. Inconsistent use of time and causal connectors in narratives.	6. Within conversation the student will produce narratives using "When" clauses to specify time relationships.
7. Limited spatial lexicon when giving directions.	7. Within conversation the student will provide directions using "right" "left" "across" and "down the ____."
8. Omits "do" in yes/no questions.	8. Within conversation the student will request information using yes/no questions that include "do".

Student Weaknesses cont'd	Objectives
9. Inconsistent use of correct verb tense; lack of auxiliary in past progressive.	9. Within conversation the student will produce a narrative using past and past progressive forms of the verb.
10. Inconsistent use of "to" in infinitives.	10. Within conversation the student will comment using the full form of the infinitive.

Attainment of these objectives by the student would greatly enhance her conversational ability.

Once the learning objectives have been determined, the teacher is ready to create the scenarios which will be the heart of instruction. Before discussing procedures for creating scenarios, two important ideas need to be presented—Learning Frame and Individualized Instruction.

Learning Frame

Effective instruction requires that learning objectives be framed within familiar contexts. Children learn best when what is to be learned is embedded within what is known. This concept was introduced in the Rationale when discussing the importance of context to the acquisition of conversational skill. It is by using context that children are able to learn language. Learning Frame was also discussed in the section on Conversational Scenarios. Specifically, all scenarios should be built on situations with which the child is thoroughly familiar. This ensures that the conversational objective to be attained is the only new element which the child has to learn.

For example, when a new FUNCTION is to be learned old FORMS should serve this purpose. Therefore, a child who is ready to begin learning to produce narratives must have mastered a wide range of two- and three-word semantic relationships before attempting this task.

When a child is expected to learn a new linguistic FORM he/she should have mastery of all the other elements of the utterance. A child who needs to learn to include the auxiliary in yes/no questions must have control of the idea to be expressed and when it is appropriate within conversation. For example, the student described on the preceding pages has all the necessary prerequisites for learning to ask, "Do you want some cake?" and "Do you want to buy?" using correct syntax. It is then appropriate to write an objective which states, "The student will request information by including the auxiliary "do" in yes/no questions." In this way the learner is using an established conversational FUNCTION (requesting information) which is very familiar. In short, children learn new linguistic forms best when those forms are serving known functions and are made up of familiar ideas.

To frame instruction effectively, the teacher needs to ascertain the strengths that each child possesses and use those strengths to develop new learning. This requires that instructions be individualized in order to give each child his or her best chance of success.

Individualizing Instruction

Acquiring conversational competence is unique for each child. Therefore it is necessary that the teacher individualize objectives and instruction. Two or more children may have very similar needs at a given time. However, individual differences in experience and in the rate of acquisition will necessitate variation in objectives and/ or instruction. This level of individualization is critical if each child is to reach his full potential.

Accomplishing the goal of individualized instruction may require restructuring of classroom management and routine so that instruction comes as close as possible to matching the ideal language learning environment—one-to-one conversation. In other words, for children to acquire conversational competence, the teacher will need to schedule individual conversation time with each child. The number of children in a class will determine the amount of time available for each child. However, it is desirable for each child to receive ten to fifteen minutes per day of individual conversation development. This time is used to work on two or three objectives. Working on two or three objectives concurrently minimizes the chance that the child will merely memorize what is to be learned.

For example, the teacher of the student whose objectives are listed on Pages 82 and 83 will work on developing the setting statement within narratives; beginning directions with a clear point of origin; and using simple sentences within explanations. One day of instruction will be made up of three scenarios—one for each objective. The next day of instruction will be made up of different scenarios addressing the same objectives. This continues until mastery of one of the objectives is attained. At that time a new objective is added. This routine continues throughout the year.

At the same time, another child in the room has different needs. He is ready to learn to use time connectors within narratives; more consistent use of pronouns to signal old information; and a wider array of lexicon when describing. His instruction will be made up of different scenarios, but will proceed on a similar schedule. Each child in the class will have a personalized set of objectives and will be learning what is most appropriate for him or her at any given time.

Individualizing instruction requires that the teacher create learning centers within the classroom. These centers will be designed so that students can engage in meaningful learning with a teacher aide and/or on their own. Working independently on reading, math and writing tasks is a constructive use of student's time. These can be paper and pencil activities or involve computers, tape recorders, language masters or other media. In some classrooms it will be necessary for one of the children to watch the teacher and a child engaged in conversational scenarios. This can be a useful and profitable activity.

Regardless of the strategies employed it is important for the teacher to manage instruction so that each student is learning what he or she needs to learn in a framework that is most appropriate. (A more complete description of strategies for implementing individualized instruction appears as Appendix C.)

Once the teacher has selected objectives which reflect child need and ability and has planned for individualizing instruction, it is time to create scenarios which will bring about attainment of the objectives. This process is discussed in the following section.

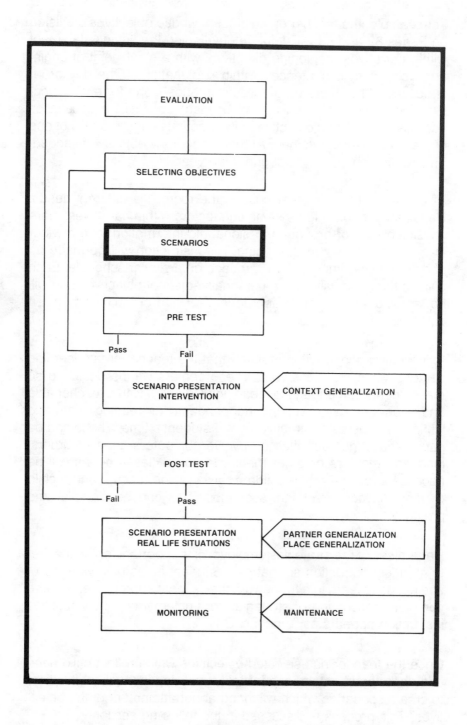

EVALUATION

SELECTING OBJECTIVES

SCENARIOS

PRE TEST

Pass | Fail

SCENARIO PRESENTATION INTERVENTION ← CONTEXT GENERALIZATION

POST TEST

Fail | Pass

SCENARIO PRESENTATION REAL LIFE SITUATIONS ← PARTNER GENERALIZATION PLACE GENERALIZATION

MONITORING ← MAINTENANCE

7 Scenarios

After objectives have been determined, but before instruction begins, the teacher must determine what conversational sequences will bring about a need for the objective. Every utterance in a conversation is predicated on the four areas of context, the intended effect of the utterance, and the partner. Therefore all of these factors need to be considered when creating Scenarios. Teachers who utilize scenarios in their teaching soon become familiar with conversational histories, i.e., the ebb and flow of everyday conversation.

Attaining an objective requires that a student engage in many scenarios which call for that objective. This is necessary to ensure that the child experiences the widest possible array of contexts possible for the objective. Planning instruction, then, is a process of creating a number of scenarios which call for the objective to be used.

For the student who needs to increase ability in providing a complete setting statement in narratives the following scenarios would be appropriate. (An example of an acceptable opening statement follows the Scenario set-up.)

1. "Let's pretend that your daddy has been away. He came home on an airplane. You and your mom went to pick him up at the airport. He brought you a present. On the way home you all went to Baskin-Robbins for ice cream. When you come to school you tell me about it."
   "Mommy and I went to the airport to get my daddy."

2. "Let's pretend that one day at recess a little kitten came on the playground. Everybody played with it. You held it. When the bell rang it got scared and ran away. When you come back in the room you tell me what happened."
   "A little kitten came on the playground."

3. "This time let's pretend you had to go to the doctor. The nurse weighed you and measured you. Then the doctor came in and looked at your throat. He gave you a shot. When you come to school you tell your friend about it."
   "Yesterday I went to the doctor with my mom."

4. "Pretend that our class went downtown to see Santa Claus. We rode the bus. Santa gave everyone a candy cane. We had some hot chocolate in a restaurant. When your daddy comes home from work you tell him about it."
   "My class went to see Santa Claus today."

5. "One Saturday you went to the park to play with your friends. You were on the swings. You were going very high. You jumped out of the swing and fell down. You scraped your knee very badly. Your mom put a big bandage on it. On Monday you come to school and tell everyone what happended."
   "On Saturday I went to the park and I fell off the swing."

For a student who is ready to learn to request information using Yes/No Questions with appropriate placement of the auxiliary i.e. "Will you . . .?" "Is she . . .?" "Do you . . .?" the scenarios listed below will be appropriate. Recall that the scenario will be presented using this language and then the teacher will check to make sure the child understands the situation before proceeding. *At no time will the teacher give the target utterance to the child.*

1. "Let's pretend that it is time for lunch. You open your lunch and see that your mom forgot to put in your thermos. You want to buy some milk, but you don't have any money. You decide to ask your friend, Nancy, if you can borrow a quarter."
"Nancy, can I borrow a quarter for milk?"

2. "Let's pretend that grandma calls you on the telephone. She wants you to come over to see her. You will have to ask your mom. I'll be grandma and mom and you be yourself."
"Can I go over to Grandma's house?"
(Note that some scenarios call for the teacher to take more than one role.)

3. "You have invited a friend to come over to your house to play. You want to play Barbies with her but you don't know if she has one. You ask her if she does. I'll be your friend."
"Do you have a Barbie?"

4. Pretend that your mom asked you to go to the store to buy some milk. You want your sister to go with you so you ask her to go. I'll be your mom and your sister."
"Will you go to the store with me?"

5. One day you are playing on the playground and you find a dollar bill. You don't know whose it is so you have to ask people. I'll be myself and you ask me about it."
"Is this yours?"

While creating scenarios it is important for the teacher to "talk through" the dialogues to be certain that the objective would naturally and logically occur. Saying the dialogue out loud or trying it out on another adult are two useful ways of checking for appropriateness. It is very easy to force a construction that really does not belong. Teachers need to be on guard so that they do not teach inappropriate or incorrect usage. A common example of this occurs when a teacher has an objective that calls for a student to produce location statements in response to questions.

For example:

> **T:** "Where did you put your lunch?"
> **C:** "I put my lunch in the closet."

Competent conversation calls for the student to respond with the needed information only, i.e., "In the closet." Another example is teaching children to say "Do you know where . . .?" when "Where is . . .?" would be more appropriate. There are times when the former would be more appropriate but those situations need to be thought out and "talked out" very carefully.

Scenarios can also be used to have a student acquire or broaden a conversational function. The following scenarios were designed to have the student learn to request information, in this case whether an action is permissible, using a variety of terms. Note that this child is functioning at a one-word expressive level and is learning to use her vocabulary in a functional manner.

1. "I will be mommy. You are Stephanie. We are at home. Everybody is playing outside. See all the kids? You want to play. I'll be here. You look out the window. Then you come and ask me."
   "Outside?"

2. "You are Kristi. I am mommy. We are at home. I am making a cake. You want to help me."
   "Stir?"

3. "I am mommy. You are Brian. We are at home. I put on my coat. I am going to the store. You want to go with me."
   "Go?"

4. "We are at school. We're on the playground. I am pushing Nicole on the swing. You want to push her. You ask me."
   "Push?"

5. "I will be Erin. You are Dina. I am playing with some blocks. You want to play. You ask me."
   "Play?"

The following scenarios were designed for a student who was ready to learn to comment using the infinite form.

1. "I'll be mom and you be Keenan. I'm getting ready to go to the store. I ask you to go with me. You don't want to go. You want to stay home and play."
   "I want to stay home."

2. "I'll be your friend, David. You be Keenan. We are outside playing. Your mom calls you in for dinner. You tell me you are going home."

"I have to go home now."

3. "You be Kevin and I'll be Alexis. You are at my house. I have a new ping-pong table. You would like to play."
"I want to play ping-pong."

4. "You be yourself and I'll be your friend Aaron. I'll come over to your house to play baseball. But, you can't play because you have a lot of homework."
"I have to do my homework."

These scenarios were created to help a student gain more consistent use of connectors when giving directions.

1. "Pretend that you are your mother and I am me. You call and invite me to dinner at your house. I don't know how to get there so you give me directions."

2. "Let's pretend that you work in the gas station on the corner. I am from Seattle and want to know how to get to Beaverton. You tell me how to get there."

A student who is ready to learn to comment using casual relationships introduced by "because" will profit from the following scenarios.

1. "Let's pretend that you are late coming to school. Your alarm clock broke and didn't wake you up. When you get to school you have to tell me what happened."
"I'm late because my alarm clock broke."

2. "Pretend that you are a Cub Scout leader. You are sick. You have to call the Cub Scouts to tell them there won't be a meeting this afternoon."
"We won't have Cub Scouts today because I am sick."

3. "Let's pretend that your mom is coming to pick you up after school. You won't be riding the bus so you tell me about that."
"I'm not riding home on the bus because my mom is coming to get me."

The following scenarios were developed to help a student increase his ability to use time connectors when explaining.

1. "Let's pretend that I am Eric and I don't know how to play "Go Fish" and you are going to tell me how."

2. "Pretend that we are at recess and you want me to play four square with you. I don't know how so you have to tell me what to do."

3. "Pretend that I am Josh. Your dad showed you how to make tacos. I don't know how so you tell me."

In all of these instances the child will need to experience additional scenarios before consistent production is achieved. The thrust of instruction is for the child to acquire a generalized conversational schema, not to memorize a series of scripts or to decipher the objective. With a generalized schema the child will express appropriate usage regardless of the context. For this to occur the child must have a variety of learning opportunities in many different conversational contexts. In this way the many conversational constraints that call for a particular utterance or series of utterances can be learned.

Once the teacher has created a number of scenarios it is time to begin instruction by giving a Pre-Test to determine and document the child's level of functioning.

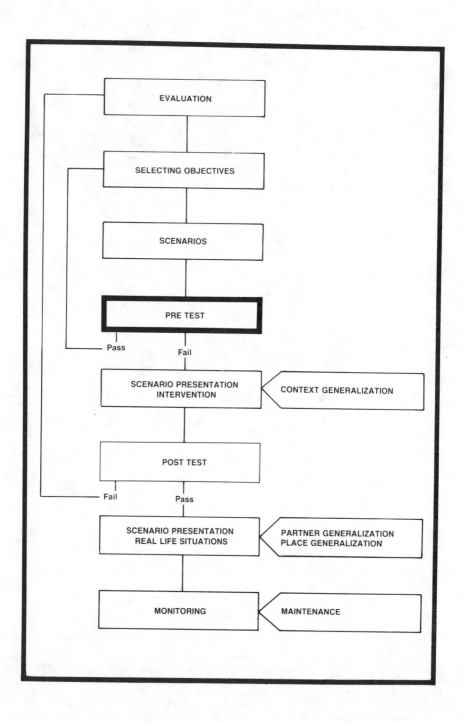

EVALUATION

SELECTING OBJECTIVES

SCENARIOS

PRE TEST

Pass — Fail

SCENARIO PRESENTATION INTERVENTION — CONTEXT GENERALIZATION

POST TEST

Fail — Pass

SCENARIO PRESENTATION REAL LIFE SITUATIONS — PARTNER GENERALIZATION PLACE GENERALIZATION

MONITORING — MAINTENANCE

8 Pre-Test

The Pre-Test is used to determine the baseline of performance against which the effectiveness of instruction will be measured. To ascertain this baseline the teacher presents three scenarios to the child and records whether the objective is produced correctly or incorrectly. No intervention is utilized during presentation of pre-test scenarios. If the child uses the objective appropriately in two or three of the scenarios, the objective should be discarded and a new objective chosen. This level of performance indicates that the objective is functional for the child and instruction is unnecessary. If the child does not use the objective or uses it correctly only once, instruction should proceed. Pre-Test scenarios are not used again until the child is ready for Post-Testing. In this way the attainment of objectives and efficacy of instruction can be clearly documented.

Pre-Testing is a critical step in the instructional process and should not be overlooked. It requires a minimal amount of time with important benefits. If the child successfully passes the teacher can select another objective and valuable instructional time is saved. Conversely, when a child fails the Pre-Test, the teacher's evaluation is validated and s/he can proceed confidently knowing that instruction is aimed toward an appropriate objective. Finally, comparing Pre-Test and Post-Test results confirms for the teacher and parents that conversational competence is growing.

Instruction Checklist

The following page presents an *Instruction Checklist* which will facilitate record keeping for each phase of instruction i.e. Pre-Test, Scenario Presentation, Post-Test and Monitoring. The left hand column is used to write the objectives to be assessed and worked on. The second column is used to indicate the score on the Pre-Test. The large central section labeled scenarios is used to indicate if the student correctly or incorrectly achieved the objective the first time possible within a scenario. The next column is used to enter the Post-Test score and the final column is to record follow-up results which will be discussed in the section on Monitoring.

Once a student has successfully used the objective in three successive scenarios it is time to discontinue instruction and introduce a new objective. Allow three days before administering the Post-Test. In this way the quality of retention is measured. Post-Testing is discussed more fully in that section.

INSTRUCTION CHECKLIST

Teacher _____

Child _____

| Objective | Pre-Test | | Scenario Presentation | | | | | | | | | | | | Post Tests | |
	Score	Date	1	2	3	4	5	6	7	8	9	10	11	12	Score/Date	Score/Date

v = Objective attained on first attempt
x = Objective attained on later attempt
o = Objective not attained

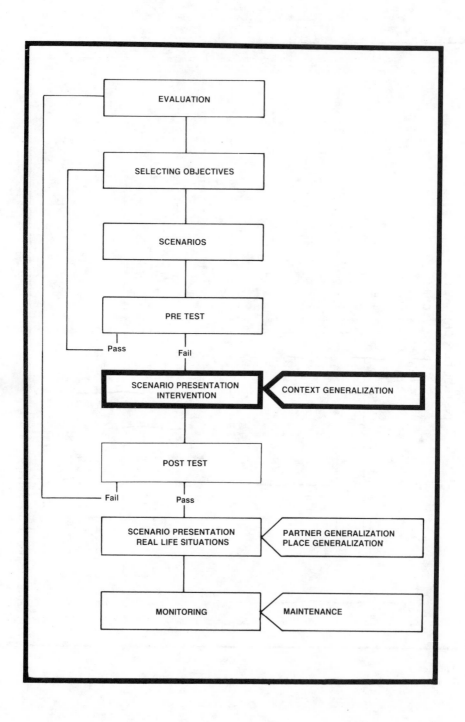

9 Scenario Presentation I/ Intervention

SCENARIO PRESENTATION

Effective Scenario Presentation depends primarily on the quality of the scenario to be presented. Every scenario must be built on situations and characters with which the student is intimately familiar. Home and school are locations containing events and persons which meet these requirements. The reader is referred to the section on Conversational Scenarios for a detailed description of the qualities of effective scenarios.

The strategies used to present a scenario to a child depend on his or her level of competence. Children just beginning with role-playing scenarios will require assistance. The following suggestions will help the teacher who is introducing scenarios for the first time:

1. Use teacher-drawn picture books which highlight the action of the scenario.
2. Use dolls or small people figures which represent a family or teacher and child to indicate to the child the roles to be played.
3. Have another adult or older child role play with the teacher while the child looks on.

Regardless of the strategies used hearing-impaired children acquire the concept of role-playing very rapidly and enjoy the process very much. The use of these augmentive strategies will not be necessary for long.

Basic Procedure

Whether using augmentive strategies or presenting scenarios verbally alone, the following procedures are used:

1. Present the scenario to the child including the setting, characters and general content of the conversation, but not the specific dialogue. *Avoid using the target language construction.*
2. Check for comprehension by questioning, e.g., "Who are you?", "Who am I?", "Where are we?", "What's the problem?", etc.
3. Begin the scenario and intervene as appropriate. (Specific intervention strategies will be discussed later in this section.)

Scheduling

To avoid having children merely memorize an objective and use it in a rote fashion they should work on two or, preferably, three objectives concurrently. For example, a student at Stage Three might be working on the following objectives at the same time:

1. Request information using "why" questions.
2. Describing using "with" phrases.
3. Commenting using "won't" and "don't".

Each objective is addressed each day in a different scenario. In other words, this child is engaged in three scenarios per day with each scenario having a single objective for which the teacher intervenes. Furthermore, since instruction is individualized, each of these objectives will be in different stages of acquisition. That is, the student may have been working on requesting information using "why" for two weeks, describing using "with" phrases for six days, and commenting using the negatives for two days. When the child has used an objective successfully on three consecutive days it is time to discontinue that objective and begin with a new one. The Post-Test will follow in three days.

All of the children in the class receive instruction on a similar schedule, but work on objectives appropriate to him/her at an individualized rate. This necessitates individualizing instruction so that each child has the benefit of working toward objectives appropriate for him or her at a pace that is likewise individualized. As objectives are individualized so too is intervention.

INTERVENTION

Intervention during scenarios should occur only for the specific instructional objective of that scenario. If the child makes an error on something other than the objective it should not be corrected during the 'scenario. Rather the tecaher should note the error and, if appropriate, schedule instruction to cover it at a later time. This avoids the problem of trying to correct too many errors at once and ensures that the scenario will maintain its conversational flow. Excessive intervening destroys the natural flow of conversation and is to be avoided.

There are four intervention strategies that when carefully used will bring about the desired learning outcomes. They are Teacher Clarification, Role-Switching, Requesting Clarification, and Prompting. Each is detailed in the following sections.

Teacher Clarification

When a child misstates the objective of the scenario a powerful intervention strategy is for the teacher to pause, give a puzzled look and say something like, "Oh you mean . . . ." and insert the correct language. The dialogue is completed and then begun again. An example will clarify this strategy. The objective of this scenario is for the student to provide a description which includes a "with" phrase. (The teacher's intervention is underlined.)

T: Let's pretend that I am your Mom and you went to the mall with your friends. You saw a beautiful dress that you want to buy. It looks like this." (Shows picture to child) "You come home and tell me all about it.

C: "O.K."

T: You go over there and pretend to come home. I'll be in the kitchen."

C: "Hi Mom."

T: (As Mom) "Hi, did you have fun at the mall?

C: "Yes. I like the red dress. White stripes on sleeve and big buttons."

T: "Oh, you mean it is red with white stripes on the sleeve and big white buttons."

C: "Yes."

T: "Oh it sounds very pretty. When I go shopping tommorrow I'll look for it."

C: "O.K."

T: "Let's start over. You pretend that you're just coming home to tell me about the dress."

C: "Mom, I'm home."

T: "Hi, did you have fun?"

C: "Yes. I saw a pretty dress. Can I buy it?"

T: "Well what does it look like?

C: "It is red with white stripes on the sleeve and big buttons."

T: "How much does it cost?"

C: "Twenty dollars."

T: "I will look for it when I go shopping tommorrow."

C: "Oh good."

In this instance the child needed only one intervention before she produced the objective. If she had needed additional intervention the teacher may have used the same strategy again or used a Role Switch or Request for Clarification which are described below.

The major strengths of this strategy are that it does little to impede the conversational flow and it does not say to the child that s/he has made an error; rather it is an attempt by the teacher to respond correctly to the content of the child's message.

Role-Switching

The second intervention strategy calls for the teacher and student to switch roles at an appropriate time during a scenario. After a child has made an error on the scenario objective, the teacher switches roles with the child and uses the desired language, giving the child a chance to respond to the objective utterance. The teacher and child then switch back to their original roles and the scenario is begun again. (For children up to the age of seven or eight physically switching places is helpful.) The following example of an eight-year-old boy with his teacher will clarify the use of Role-Switching. In this scenario the objective is an appropriate setting statement within a narrative. (The entire Role Switch is underlined.)

T: "Let's pretend that you went camping with your Boy Scout troop last Saturday on Mt. Hood. You slept in tents and went hiking and fishing. You didn't catch any fish but your friend Bill did. He let you take one home. On Monday you come into school and tell me about your trip."

C: "O.K." (Walks to classroom door and pretends to come in.) "Good morning."

T: "Hi. Did you have a good weekend?"

C: "I went camping. I didn't catch any fish. Bill caught five fish. He gave one to me. I took it home."

T: "Wow, that's very nice. He's a good friend."

C: Yeah."

T: "Let's switch."

T: (As student) "Good morning."

C: (As teacher) "Hi, how are you."

T: "Fine. Guess what."

C: "What?"

T: "Last Saturday I went camping with my Boy Scout troop on Mt. Hood. We slept in tents and went hiking and fishing. I didn't catch any fish. Bill caught five fish. He gave me one. I took it home."

C: "Oh, that's very nice."

T: "O.K. Let's switch back. You be yourself and I'll be me."

C: (Pretends to come in the door.) "Hi."

T: "Hi. How was your weekend?"

C: I went camping on Mt. Hood with the Boy Scouts. I didn't catch any fish. Bill caught five fish. He gave me one fish. I took it home."

T: "Wow! That sounds like fun."
C: "Yeah. I like camping."

In this scenario the child needed only one role switch to significantly improve his setting statement. If he had not improved with one Role Switch the teacher would have switched again and kept switching until the child improved his production. Note also that the teacher accepted an improved version of the setting statement and moved on. He did not intervene to attempt to improve other aspects of the narrative. Those objectives will come later when the child has better mastery of the setting statement.

The strengths of this strategy are (1) the child has an opportunity to hear the correct language in full context and must respond to it appropriately; 2) s/he must process this language in such a way that it is held in memory for a time; and 3) s/he must attempt to use the correct language once the scenario is enacted again. Role-Switching may be done a number of times within a scenario.

Role-Switching is a very important and effective strategy. It eliminates simple parroting of correct language by placing the child in the position of having to retain the appropriate language and then use it. This has decided advantages over the modeling of correct language with an immediate imitation by the student. It is the most commonly used strategy for helping children develop appropriate conversational skills. It can be used successfully with all ages of school children and for objectives from the Structure, Function and Form areas.

Requesting Clarification

Like teacher clarification, this strategy maintains conversational flow very well. It involves letting the child know that his/her utterance is not adequate and waiting for the child to repair it. This can be accomplished by the teacher saying. "Pardon me.", "What?", "What did you say?", "I didn't hear that." etc. Clarification can also be requested by looking quizzically at the child. An example of requesting clarification follows. In this scenario the objective is for the student to comment using a When clause to specify a time relationship. (The intervention is underlined.)

C: "I was at the store. I saw Mary and Bill."

T: "What was that?"
C: "When I was at the store I saw Mary and Bill."
T: "Oh, really. What were they doing?"

The strength of this strategy is that it places responsibility for improving communication effectiveness on the child. In addition, it is a strategy commonly used by parents with their normally developing children. The nature of this strategy dictates that it will be used when the child is approaching mastery of the objective.

Prompt

Only one situation calls for this strategy which requires the teacher to step out of the role of conversational partner and into the teacher role. This arises when the child has used a language construction which is correct, but could be more appropriately or efficiently spoken. When this occurs the teacher can say, "That is O.K., but can you think of another way to say it?" If the child can use a more mature form the scenario should be started over again so that the child has an opportunity to practice the utterance within a conversational context.

If the child is unable to self-correct the utterance the teacher can say, "That was all right, but there is something else you could have said." and then Role Switch and begin the scenario again. An example of the appropriate use of this strategy occurs in the following scenario which was designed to increase the number of times this student requests information. (The prompt is underlined.)

T: "Let's pretend you are playing outside and you find a little brown box. You want to open it but you can't get it open. You bring it into the house and ask me to open it. I'll be mom and I'll be in the kitchen."
C: "O.K." (Child mdoves away and pretend to be playing outside. She picks up an imaginary box and tries to open it. Failing, she goes into the house.) "Mom, I find a box."
T: (As Mom) "Oh, let me see."
C: "I can't open."
T: "Mmmm. Let me see." (Looks at box, turns it over and then pretends to open it.) "Here you go. I got it."
C: "Oh, thank you."
T: "You're welcome."

C: "I go play."

T: "That was O.K. but there is something else you might say. Let's start over. I'll be you and you be Mom."

T: (As Child) "Mom, I found a box outside but I can't open it."

C: (As Mom) "I will open for you." (Opens box.)

T: "Oh, how did you open it?"

C: "Mmmm. I'm strong."

T: "O.K. Let's switch."

C: "Look Mom. I find a box. I can't open."

T: "Let me see. Maybe I can open it for you." (Pretends to look over box and pushes imaginary button on the bottom.) "There it's open."

C: "How you open box?"

T: "Well, I saw this little button on the bottom and I pushed it. Then the box opened."

C: "Thank you Mommy."

T: "You're welcome."

In this example the Prompt was used to increase the use of the conversational intent of requesting information. Prompts may also be used when a child has used a correct but immature or less complex language form than is deemed appropriate by the teacher. Care needs to be taken to use this strategy only for constructions that are appropriate within the conversation.

Summary and Examples

Each of these intervention strategies has proven successful with children of varying ages and abilities. Selecting intervention strategies requires the same individualization that goes into selecting objectives and designing scenarios. The teacher should always choose the least disruptive strategy that works for each child. Student learning style and ability are crucial variables which the teacher will take into account when intervening. Careful evaluation by the teacher of child progress will lead to an appropriate blend of strategies.

The following dialogues contain additional examples of appropriate use of intervention strategies.

Example One

This scenario was designed to help a five-year-old student learn to produce a negative comment using "can't". This is Day Three of instruction. (All interventions are underlined.)

T: "Today let's pretend that you are you and I am your Mom. We're at home on your farm. You've been playing outside. It's very muddy. You have on your boots. You come in the house and take off your coat. You try to take off your boots but they are stuck. They won't come off. You pull and pull but they won't come off. You'll have to ask Mom for help. I'll be Mom. I'll be in the living room reading a book."

C: "O.K."

S: "Do you understand?"

C: "Yes."

S: "Who are you?"

C: "Me."

S: "And where are we?"

C: "On the farm."

T: "Good. Let's start."

C: (Pretends to come in the house. Takes off her coat and sits down to take off her boots. After struggling for a few seconds she calls for help.) "Mom."

T: (As Mom) "What?"

C: "Come here."

T: "Coming." (Gets up and walks over to where the student is struggling.) "What's the problem?"

C: "I (shake head) off boot. Hard."

T: "Oh, you can't take off your boots." (Teacher Clarification) "Here, I'll help you."

C: "Thank you."

T: "You're welcome."

T: "O.K. Let's switch. You be mom and I'll be you." (Role Switch.)

T: (As student, comes into the house, hangs up her coat and struggles with her boots.) "Mom."

C: (As Mom) "What?"

T: "Please come here."

C: "O.K." (Walks over to teacher.) "What's wrong?"

T: "I can't take off my boots."

C: "Oh, I help you." (Reaches down and pulls off boots.)

T: "Thank you."

C: "You're welcome.."

T: "Now, you be yourself again and I'll be Mom." (End of Role Switch.)

C: "O.K."

C: (Pretends to come in the house, hangs up her coat and sits down to take off her boots. Struggles with her boots and calls for help.) "Mom."

T: "What?"

C: "Come help me."

T: (Walks over to student.) "What wrong?"

C; "I can't off boot."

T: "Oh, you can't take off your boots. (Teacher Clarification) I'll help you." (Pulls off boots.) "There you go."

C: "Thank you."

T: "You're welcome."

T: "Thank you. You worked very hard today."

The teacher used two of the intervention strategies during this instructional sequence. Note how the Teacher Clarification did not impede the flow of conversation. Also note that the Role Switch was begun when the first dialogue was complete. During the final dialogue the student used "can't" appropriately; however she did not include the verb. She stills needs more work on this linguistic form and does acquire the objective in the next example.

Example Two

The following example is the fifth day of instruction on this objective. (Interventions are underlined.)

T: "Today let's pretend that we are at home. I'll be Mom. We're in the kitchen. You are helping me fix lunch. You get the peanut butter and jam. You open the jam but the peanut butter lid is stuck. It won't open. You try and try, but it won't open. You ask me to help you."

C: "O.K."

T: "Where are we?"

C: "Home."

T: "Right. Who am I?"
C: "Mom."
T: "Let's start."
T: (As Mom) "Will you please help me fix lunch?"
C: "Sure." (Both pretend to walk into the kitchen.)
T: "Please get the peanut butter and jam. I'll get the bread."
C: (Pretends to get peanut butter and jam. Opens jam and then struggles with peanut butter.) "I can't peanut butter."
T: What was that?" (Requesting Clarification)
C: "I can't peanut butter."
T: "Oh, you can't open it. (Teacher Clarification) Let me try."
C: "Here."
T: (Opens jar and hands it back.) "Here you are."
T: Let's switch." (Role Switch)
C: (As Mom) "Please help me. Lunch."
T: (As child) "O.K."
C: "You get jam and peanut butter."
T: (Gets jam and peanut butter. Opens jam and struggles with peanut butter.) "I can't open peanut butter."
C: "I will."
T: "Now, let's switch back. You be you and I'll be Mom." (end of Role Switch)
T: (As Mom) "Will you please help me fix lunch?"
C: "O.K." (Both walk into the kitchen.)
T: "You get the peanut butter and jam. I'll get the bread and potato chips."
C: (Gets the peanut butter and jam. Opens jam and struggles with the peanut butter.) "I can't open the peanut butter."
T: "Oh dear, let me help you."
T: "You worked hard today. Thank you."

In this instructional sequence the student spontaneously used "can't" correctly without intervention. However, she needed a Role Switch before she used the complete verb phrase. During subsequent scenarios she used the appropriate form without teacher intervention. When she had done this on three consecutive days, instruction was discontinued. The Post-Test was administered three days later. Post-Testing is described fully in the next section. Before moving on Extended Turn Intervention and Context Generalization will be discussed.

Extended Turn Intervention

Developing competence with extended turns within conversations requires some modifications of the basic procedure for Scenario Presentation and Intervention. For children who have not developed narrative skills the following activities are helpful:

1. Give the child the full narrative verbally. Then, with the child playing his role, act out the entire story. Then proceed with the scenario having the child relate the narrative. This strategy is useful until the child has acquired the ability to take in a narrative verbally and then relate it.

2. With parental cooperation, determine narratives that the child can relate which are real experiences for the child. Intervention proceeds in the same manner as with all scenarios.

3. Have the child relate narratives that he has completed with the teacher to other persons who are totally unfamiliar with the story.

With direction-giving it is helpful to have the child walk out the directions they are to give or to trace them on a map before the scenario begins. The purpose of the scenarios is to provide the child opportunities to learn to express a set of directions with which he is very familiar. By engaging in these pre-scenario activities the teacher can be certain that the child's ability to express directions is being developed to its fullest. Other areas of the curriculum can provide valuable experiences for developing direction-giving skill. Social studies activities built on neighborhoods—the school and the child's—provide excellent material for direction-giving scenarios.

Children just beginning to give explanations need to have the materials at hand that are used in the explanation. In this way the teacher can be confident that the conversational skill of explaining is the only variable facing the child. They can go through the stages before beginning the scenario. This allows the teacher to be certain that the child is only working on acquiring the skill of giving an explanation, not learning how to do something which will then be explained. Science and math are areas of the curriculum which provide a wealth of material for children learning to explain. Telling how to play different games is also very useful when working on explanations.

Children just beginning to work on descriptions profit from having a picture or real object to look at before the scenario is begun. The goal always is to ensure that the child has sufficient experience to make the scenario a conversational skill activity first and foremost. Many real-life situations lend themselves to describing scenarios. The opening of school is a wonderful time to have children increase their ability by describing new school clothes which they have yet to wear. The time following Christmas can be used to have children describe gifts they and other family members received.

Children develop the ability to use extended turns best when they are based on real and common experiences. Extended turns are such a critical component of effective conversational skill that they merit intense work by the teacher to make them fully functional for their students.

An important component of making extended turns functional is to have children practice them with other adults and children who are unfamiliar with the content. Classroom visitors, other staff members and other students are readily available resources. Parents are very interested persons who will make good conversational partners for extended turns. These strategies are the beginnings of establishing generalization of learning which is described in detail in the following section.

Context Generalization

Insufficient attention is given to the concept and practice of generalizing the language learning of hearing-impaired children. Too often instruction is carried on in the classroom within a closed set of conditions with the expectation that whatever is learned will be used productively in other situations. This approach to instruction leaves the most critical aspect of learning - practical living use - to chance. The inefficiency and ineffectiveness of this practice dictates that specific steps be taken to ensure generalization of learning. The first step of developing context generalization is for children to learn langue within a conversational setting. In this way the child understands immediately that language is used to communicate ideas and feelings to others and is not merely an academic exercise. The corollary to this is that children need to experience the skills they are acquiring in a wide variety of conversations. This means that each objective will be addressed in a sufficient number of scenarios so that the child can induce the many constraints on correct usage.

It is equally important that the teacher be aware of additional opportunities within the classroom for enhancing context generalization. The many conversations that occur throughout the day are ideal for this. The intervention strategies of Teacher Clarification and Requesting Clarification are ways of providing opportunities for acquiring context generalization without impeding the natural flow of conversation.

Once the student has used the instructional objective in three consecutive scenarios it is time to discontinue instruction and prepare for Post-Testing which is described in the following section.

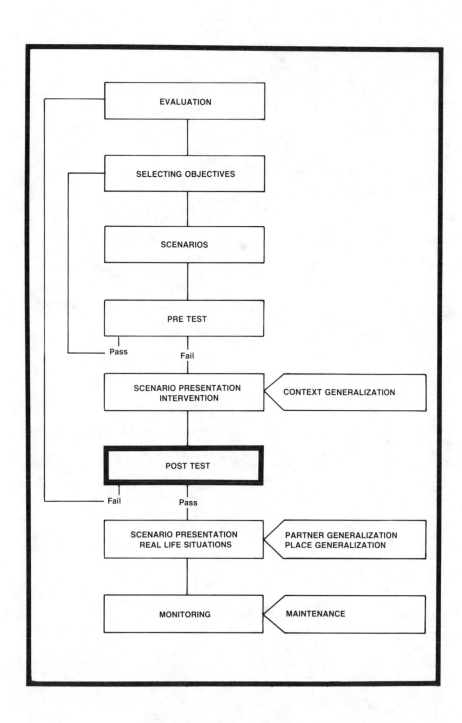

EVALUATION

SELECTING OBJECTIVES

SCENARIOS

PRE TEST

Pass Fail

SCENARIO PRESENTATION
INTERVENTION

CONTEXT GENERALIZATION

POST TEST

Fail Pass

SCENARIO PRESENTATION
REAL LIFE SITUATIONS

PARTNER GENERALIZATION
PLACE GENERALIZATION

MONITORING

MAINTENANCE

10 Post-Test

The Post-Test consists of presenting the scenarios used in the Pre-Test to determine if the child can now use the objective appropriately. If instruction has been effective the student will use the newly acquired conversational skill accurately and efficiently.

Post-Testing is initiated following a three-day delay after the student's successful use of the objective on three consecutive days of instruction. The Post-Test is delayed to ensure that long-term learning has taken place. When the Post-Test is administered immediately following several days of instruction the student may use the objective correctly in much the same fashion as students who have crammed for a final exam. That is, the knowledge is available for a short time only and is not a functional component of the child's conversational ability.

The results of the Post-Test determine subsequent action. Correct usage of the objective on two or three of the test scenarios is sufficient attainment to begin to focus on the objective in real life situations and on second stage scenarios which are detailed in the following section.

If a child does not pass the Post-Test the teacher must determine the cause. Reasons for not passing the Post-Test correspond with the major steps of the Planning/Instruction model. Specifically:

1. The Evaluation may have overestimated the student's ability and important precursors may be lacking.
2. The teacher may have selected an objective for which the child was not ready.
3. The scenarios used by the teacher were not sufficiently representative of the conversational constraints necessary for the child to induce appropriate usage.
4. The child may need more experience with the objective in additional scenarios.

Regardless of the cause of lack of attainment it is essential that the teacher ascertain the probable cause and adjust teaching accordingly.

Post-Test results are recorded on the Instruction Checklist described in the Pre-Test section and become a permanent record of the child's growth.

When the child has attained mastery as indicated by the Post-Test s/he is ready to move to the next stage of instruction which focuses on broadening use of the newly acquired skill.

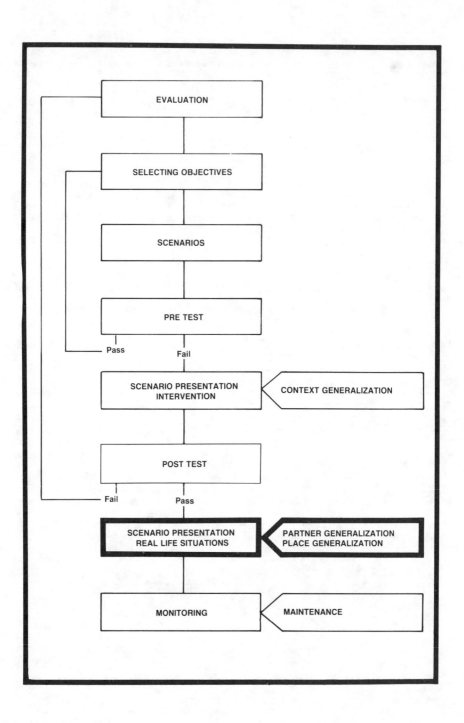

EVALUATION

SELECTING OBJECTIVES

SCENARIOS

PRE TEST

Pass   Fail

SCENARIO PRESENTATION
INTERVENTION   CONTEXT GENERALIZATION

POST TEST

Fail   Pass

SCENARIO PRESENTATION
REAL LIFE SITUATIONS   PARTNER GENERALIZATION
                       PLACE GENERALIZATION

MONITORING   MAINTENANCE

11 Scenario Presentations II/ Real-Time Scenarios

Once a child has passed the Post-Test indicating that s/he can use the objective with the teacher in a variety of linguistic contexts it is necessary to systematically broaden use to include different conversational partners and settings. This is accomplished by repeating old scenarios with different persons and utilizing real-time scenarios. The outcome of these activities is Partner and Place Generalization. Other school personnel, visitors and most importantly, parents, play a key role in this process.

Scenario Presentations II

Having different persons repeat previously completed scenarios with the child is an effective means of achieving partner generalization. Teacher aides are usually the most readily available new partner. By repeating scenarios that were used to bring the child to mastery the teacher aide can provide a valuable learning experience—conversational skills can be used with people other than the classroom teacher. The aide should use similar language in setting up the scenarios and should be trained to use the intervention strategies appropriately. Children's performance should be tracked and reported to the teacher on a regular basis. Other personnel within the school and even older students can be used to carry out partner generalization activities as well. Classroom visitors can also be a useful resource in achieving partner generalization. They can be surreptiously primed to make statements or ask questions that will elicit the desired conversational skill.

Achieving partner generalization is critical if children are to use the objective productively in their spontaneous conversations. A major strength of using this conversational approach is that children learn new skills in a functional context which facilitates transfer. All instruction requires a generalization component and using conversation as the primary vehicle of instruction makes generalizing activities readily available.

Using newly acquired conversational skills in locales other than the classroom (Place Generalization) can be accomplished by the teacher aide working on old scenarios in other places e.g. the hallway, the school library, or the playground.

The teacher can facilitate acquisition of Partner and Place Generalization by having children relate narratives or any of the other extended turns to office personnel or other teachers. Using scenarios more than once with other people and in different locations brings about generalization that is crucial to the acquisition of conversational competence. The teacher can also utilize Real-Time Scenarios as described below.

Real-Time Scenarios

The teacher can use situations that occur throughout the day as generalization opportunities. Numerous opportunities arise that call for a child to have conversational interaction with various individuals. For example when a child needs to go to the office to request supplies or deliver a message, practicing the interaction ahead of time using the intervention strategies discussed earlier is very effective. In the following example the teacher needs some staples and wants her nine-year-old student to go get some in the office. (The intervention is underlined.)

T: "Will you please go to the office and get us some more staples from Mrs. R?"

C: "Sure."

T: "Let's practice. I'll be Mrs. R."

C: "O.K." (Pretends to walk up to teacher who is pretending to type.) "We need more staples."

T: "All right. Here's some."

C: "Thank you."

T: "You're welcome."

T: "Let's switch. I'll be you and you be Mrs. R. Pretend that you are typing."

S: "O.K.."

T: (As student) "Excuse me."

S: (As Mrs. R.) "Yes."

T: "Our staples are all gone. May we have more?"

S: "Yes. Here"

T: "Thank you."

S: "You're welcome."

T: "Let's start over."

S: (Teacher pretends to be typing and student walks up to her.) "Excuse me."

T: "Yes. Can I help you?"

S: "Yes. The staples are all gone. May I have more?"

T: "Sure. Here you go."

S: "Thank you."

T: "You're welcome."

In this example the teacher used a Role Switch within a real-time scenario to have the student practice an important politeness routine. She can check with the school secretary later in the day to ascertain if the student carried over the politeness routine to real use.

Real-time scenarios can also be used to have a child practice newly acquired linguistic forms. In the following example the teacher has determined that one of her students, who had just passed a Post-Test on requesting using well-formed yes/no questions, needs a new ear hook for his hearing aid. She asks him to go to the audiologist and get one. (The intervention is underlined.)

> **T:** "Please go to Miss A. and ask her for a new ear hook for your hearing aid. This one is broken."
> **S:** "A new ear hook?"
> **T:** "Yes. This one has a crack. See."
> **S:** "O.K."
> **T:** "Let's practice. I'll be Miss A. You come into my office."
> **S:** "Hi."
> **T:** (As Miss A.) "Hi, how are you?"
> **S:** "Fine."
> **T:** "Good."
> **S:** "I have a new ear hook?"
> **T:** "Pardon me."
> **S:** "May I have a new ear hook?"
> **T:** "O.K. Here you are."
> **S:** "Thank you."
> **T:** "You're welcome."
> "Let's start over. You be yourself and I'll be Miss A."
> You walk over there and pretend to come into my office."
> **S:** "O.K. (Walks away, turns around and walks back to the teacher.) "Hi."
> **T:** "Hi. What can I do for you today?"
> **S:** "May I have a new ear hook?"
> **T:** "Sure. Here you go."
> **S:** "Thank you."
> **T:** "You're welcome."

In this instance a teacher request for clarification was the only intervention necessary to improve this child's request. Starting the scenario over and having the child complete the dialogue correctly is an important step and should not be overlooked. Later the teacher can check with the audiologist to see if the child used appropriate language when making his request.

Daily interactions provide numerous opportunities to practice all of the extended turns. The following Real-Time Scenario is a common example of a Monday morning exchange. The student has had an exciting weekend and is anixous to share it with her teacher.

> **S:** (Coming into the classroom before school.) "Hi."

T: "Hi. How was your weekend?"

S: "Fine. You know what?"

T: "What?"

S: "I went roller skating. Billy (her brother) fell down. "I didn't fall down."

T: "Oh, that sounds like fun. Where did you go?"

S: "Oaks Park."

T: "Did you mom and dad go too?"

S: "Just daddy."

T: "Oh, I see. Let's switch."

T: (As student) "Guess what."

S: (As teacher) "What?"

T: "My dad and Billy and I went roller skating at Oaks Park. Bill fell down but I didn't fall. It was lots of fun."

S: "Did mom go?"

T: No. She stayed home."

T: Let's switch back. You come in and tell me what happened."

S: "Guess what. Daddy and Billy and I went roller skating. Billy fell down. I didn't fall down."

T: "Wow. That sounds like fun."

By planning for additional practice with other persons of scenarios and careful use of intervention during real-life conversations the teacher can significantly increase each student's conversational competence. Involving parents in the conversational development process is the most effective means teachers have for ensuring the success of instruction.

Parents as Generalization Agents

Parents are the most important allies that the child and teacher have in acquiring conversational competence. No one can be a more interested or caring conversation partner. Parents are most anxious to receive specific guidance on how to help their child. In traditional language programs this is not possible because of the didactic nature of instruction. That is, children are being "taught" language rather than being immersed in situations which allow them to "learn" language. The distinction is an important one, for when children learn language within a conversational model, the parents are able to have significant impact.

First of all, parents need to be aware of the role of conversation and have a basic understanding of conversational framework. It is not enought to merely tell parents to "Talk, Talk, Talk," to their children. They must know the importance of conversation and how they can enhance its development.

A variety of strategies can be used to involve parents in the instructional process. They can be informed on a weekly basis of the objectives being worked on and the objectives that have been attained. Just by knowing what has been learned parents can have an influence on their child's generalization. This can be coupled with asking parents to track appropriate use of an objective for a specific period of time. Some children and parents enjoy re-creating scenarios at home. But this should be done only after an objective has been mastered.

In their role as conversational partners it is critical that parents expose their children to all of the extended turns on a continual basis. Parents who habitually tell their children about the events of their day using well-formed narratives will significantly enhance this skill in their children. This holds true for each of the other extended turns as well. When parents explain activities that are about to happen; provide directions for the many trips taken in the family car; and give vivid descriptions of items, they are contributing significantly to their child's conversational development. The teacher's responsibility is to be certain that each parent is aware of the nature and importance of these activities and how they can be implemented in a natural way.

Parents can be taught to use two of the intervention strategies described earlier. The importance of maintaining conversational flow dictates that Teacher Clarification (in this case Parent Clarification) and Requesting Clarification are the only intervention strategies that parents should employ. For parents to understand when and how to intervene effectively requires an explanation by the teacher, practice by the parent(s) and periodic conferences to evaluate progress. Parents can facilitate conversational growth when they are given the information they need.

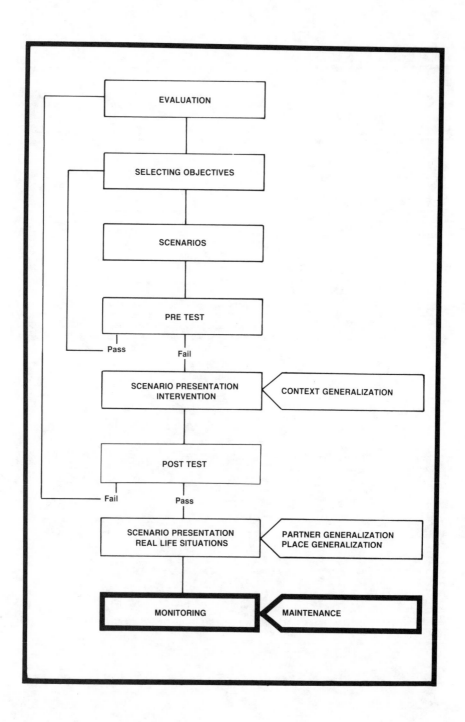

EVALUATION

SELECTING OBJECTIVES

SCENARIOS

PRE TEST

Pass   Fail

SCENARIO PRESENTATION
INTERVENTION   CONTEXT GENERALIZATION

POST TEST

Fail   Pass

SCENARIO PRESENTATION
REAL LIFE SITUATIONS   PARTNER GENERALIZATION
                                PLACE GENERALIZATION

MONITORING   MAINTENANCE

12 Monitoring

The final and ongoing step in the instructional process is tracking continued use of attained objectives. It is essential for the teacher to know if conversational skills learned in September are still productive in January or June. The Instruction Checklist on Page 97 can be used to track retention. There is room on the form to note one occurrence of usage following the Post-Test. This tracking can be done formally or informally.

Formal Monitoring is accomplished by re-doing one or two of the scenarios that were used during instruction or one of the pre- or post-test scenarios. The first such review should be done a month or so following attainment and another three months later. If the skill continues to be productive it is safe to assume that it is firmly entrenched as a part of the child's repertoire. Informal Monitoring can be accomplished by periodically reviewing the Instruction Checklist and noting whether the child has recently used skills attained earlier.

Monitoring is a very important component of instruction. Teachers commonly report that many previously acquired skills are lost to the child after a period of time. When this occurs instruction is invalidated and has actually been a waste of everyone's time. If certain skills are important enough to be taught in the first place, surely they are important enough to Monitor to ensure that they remain useful to the child. Otherwise, much time and energy has been wasted. Teachers, let alone their students, can not afford for this to occur.

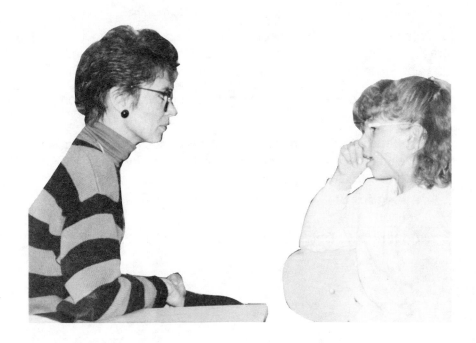

Conclusion

Developing the conversational competence of hearing-impaired children is the most challenging instructional task faced by teachers anywhere. To achieve this goal teachers must:

1. Have a thorough knowledge of the development of conversation;

2. Have an understanding of the framework of conversation; and

3. Follow systematic planning and instructional procedures.

The material presented here provides a foundation in each of these areas. By assimilating and accommodating these concepts, and by practicing and refining these strategies, the teacher will move toward developing the conversational competence of each hearing-impaired child in his or her charge.

No one text, however, can supply all the information and skills needed to achieve this goal. The reader is encouraged to continue to study the development of each child and the ever widening amount of research data and to incorporate this new data into teaching practice. Only in this way can we hope to reach the goal each of us has set for ourselves and for our students.

The appendices that follow contain additional information on key concepts and strategies.:

Appendix A: Examples of evaluation scenarios along with evaluation comments and completed Conversational Competence Evaluation forms.

Appendix B: Examples of scenario presentation and intervention.

Appendix C: Detailed strategies for individualizing instruction.

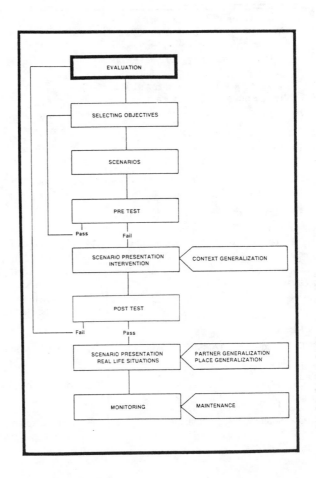

14 Appendix A

This Appendix presents additional examples of Evaluation scenarios along with comments, completed Conversational Competence Evaluation Forms and listing of objectives.

STUDENT ONE Evaluation Scenario One— Narrative	Comments on Evaluation Scenario One— Narrative
T1 "In this one I'll be your teacher and you be you. You come to school with a cast on your arm. You broke you arm. You were riding your bike. A dog ran in front of you and you fell. Your mom took you to the hospital. The doctor put a cast on your arm."	
C1 "O.K."	**C1** Acknowledged understanding of scenario.
T2 "You walk over there and pretend to come in the room."	
C2 (Child goes to door and pretends to come in.)	**C2** Responded to request for action.
T3 "Oh my goodness. What happened to your arm?"	
C3 "On my bike. A dog. I fall down."	**C3** Answered request for information. Provided informative, but poorly formed narrative. Setting is incomplete. Problem is not clearly stated. Inconsistent use of sentences.
T4 "Oh no."	
C4 "Dog run away fast."	**C4** Added a comment.
T5 "Oh dear."	
C5 "Arm hurt."	**C5** Added a comment.
T6 "I'm sorry."	
C6 "Mommy me go hospital."	**C6** Added a comment. Attempted conjoining, but left out "and". Left "to" out of location.
T7 "How long will you have to wear the cast?"	
C7 "Wait six days."	**C7** Answered request for information.
T8 "Well, you have to be more careful."	
C8 "Yes."	**C8** Acknowledged comment.

STUDENT ONE Evaluation Scenario Two— Narrative	Comments on Evaluation Scenario Two— Narrative
T1 Let's pretend that I am your friend. You went camping with your family. One night you were sleeping in your tent. A bear came. He knocked over a garbage can. He wanted food. Everybody was afraid. You come home and tell me about it."	
C1 "O.K."	**C1** Acknowledged understanding of scenario.
T2 "I'll be here playing. You come over and talk to me."	
C2 (Moves away and then walks over to teacher.) "Hi."	**C2** Initiated conversation.
T3 "Hi. How are you?"	
C3 "Fine. I camping. In sleeping bag. I hear bear. Shh. Bear look food. I hear bear."	**C3** Answered request for information. Introduced topic. Provided informative, but poorly formed narrative. Incomplete setting. Lack of resolution.
T4 "Oh no. What did you do?"	
C4 "Look. No more bear."	**C4** Answered request for information. Used negative form.
T5 "Where was he?"	
C5 "Bear run away."	**C5** Answered request for information. Incorrect verb tense.
T6 "Oh. Well I'm glad you are all right."	
C6 "Yeah."	**C6** Acknowledged comment.

STUDENT ONE Evaluation Scenario Three— Directions	Comments on Evaluation Scenario Three— Directions
T1 This time I will be a delivery person bringing books to school. I want to take them to the library. You are Mrs. B. in the office. I will ask you where the library is."	
C1 "O.K."	**C1** Acknowledged understanding of scenario.
T2 "Who are you?"	
C2 "Mrs. B."	**C2** Answered request for information.
T3 "Right. And where are we?"	
C3 "Office."	**C3** Answered request for information.
T4 "O.K. Let's start." (Pretending to carry large box.) "Excuse me."	
C4 "Hi."	**C4** Responded to initiation.
T5 "Hi. These books are for the library. Can you tell me where it is?"	
C5 "Over there." (Points)	**C5** Provided inadequate directions. Lack of point of origin. Insufficient information.
T6 "What?"	
C6 "Around upstairs. By the library."	**C6** Responded to request for clarification by giving more information. Used two more locative terms.
T7 "Oh. Thank you."	
C7 "You're welcome."	**C7** Used appropriate social routine for ending.

STUDENT ONE Evaluation Scenario Four— Explanation	Comments on Evaluation Scenario Four— Explanation
T1 "O.K. I'm your friend, Kevin. We are in the lunch room. You have a peanut butter and jam sandwich. I don't know how to make one so I will ask you how to do it."	
C1 "O.K."	**C1** Acknowledged understanding of scenario. **C2** Responded appropriately to initiation.
T3 "Do you want to sit with me?"	
C3 "O.K."	**C3** Answered request for information.
T4 "I have a turkey sandwich. What kind do you have?"	
C4 "Peanut butter jam sandwich."	**C4** Answered request for information. Attempted conjoining, but left out "and".
T5 "Oh I like those. Did you make it?"	
C5 "Yes."	**C5** Answered request for information.
T6 "How did you do that?"	
C6 "Bread. And jam. And peanut butter. And bread. Finish."	**C6** Provided explanation consisting only of list of ingredients. Did not include verbs. Used "and" as connector.
T7 "Oh that sounds easy. I'm going to make one for my lunch tomorrow."	

STUDENT ONE Evaluation Scenario Five— Description	Comments on Evaluation Scenario Five— Description
T1 "Let's pretend that I am your mom. You went to the store with your friend. You saw a toy car. You want to buy it. You come home and tell me about it.	
C1 "Toy car?"	**C1** Requested clarification.
T2 "Yes."	
C2 "O.K."	**C2** Acknowledged response to request for clarification.
T3 "Let's start. You come in the house from the store."	
C3 (pretends to come in door.) "Hi Mom."	**C3** Initiated conversation.
T4 "Hi. Did you have fun?"	
C4 "I want new car."	**C4** Introduced topic with comment. (Request would have been more polite.)
T5 "Oh, did you see one at the store?"	
C5 "Yes. I want fast car."	**C5** Answered request for information. Added comment.
T6 "Well, I don't know."	
C6 "I want buy."	**C6** Commented. Attempted use of infinitive.
T7 "What kind of car is it?"	
C7 "Fast car. Race car."	**C7** Answered request for information.
T8 "What does it look like?"	
C8 "Blue, white, yellow."	**C8** Provided description by listing colors.
T9 "How much does it cost?"	
C9 "Twelve dollar."	**C9** Answered request for information.
T10 "I'll ask your dad. Maybe you can have it."	
C10 "Daddy not home."	**C10** Commented. Used negative term.
T11 "I know. We'll ask him when he comes home from work."	
C11 "O.K."	**C11** Acknowledged comment.

STUDENT ONE Evaluation Scenario Six— Conversation	Comments on Evaluation Scenario Six— Conversation
T1 Let's pretend that I am your friend, Alexis. I'm going to call you on the phone. I want you to go to a movie with me. You will have to ask your Mom if you can go. I'll be your Mom too."	
C1 "O.K."	**C1** Acknowledged understanding of scenario.
T2 "Ring. Ring."	
C2 "Hello."	**C2** Initiated appropriately.
T3 "Hi. This is Alexis."	
C3 "Hi."	**C3** Responded to initiation.
T4 "Do you want to go to a movie with me?"	
C4 "Yes. I ask Mom."	**C4** Answered request for information. Added comment.
C5 "Mom. I go movie?"	**C5** Initiated new conversation. Requested information. Omitted auxiliary.
T5 (As Mom) "When?"	
C6 "Today."	**C6** Answered request for information.
T6 "No. I'm sorry. We are going to Grandma's house."	
C7 (To Alexis) "Mom say, 'No.' "	**C7** Commented. Used direct discourse.
T7 "Oh. Why not?"	
C8 "I go grandma house."	**C8** Answered request for information. Incorrect verb tense. Omitted locative "to".
T8 "Oh well. Maybe we can go tomorrow."	
C9 "O.K."	**C9** Acknowledged comment.
T9 "I will call you. Good-bye."	
C10 "Bye."	**C10** Ended appropriately.

STUDENT ONE Evaluation Scenario Seven— Conversation	Comments on Evaluation Scenario Seven— Conversation
T1 "I will be your Mom and you be yourself. Pretend that you went over to see your friend, Brian. He has four new puppies. You want to have one. You come home and ask me if you can have one."	
C1 "O.K."	**C1** Acknowledged understanding of scenario.
T2 "Let's start."	
C2 (Goes to door and pretends to come in.) "Mom."	**C2** Initiated appropriately.
T3 "What?"	
C3 "Brian have four puppy."	**C3** Introduced topic by commenting.
T4 "Oh, how nice."	
C4 "I have puppy?"	**C4** Requested information. Omitted auxiliary.
T5 "Oh, I don't know. What will you feed it?"	
C5 "Dog food. Water. And bone."	**C5** Answered request for information. Used one connector.
T6 "Umm. What color are the puppies?"	
C6 "Brown."	**C6** Answered request for information.
T7 "Well, we'll have to talk to your dad."	
C7 "Where daddy?"	**C7** Requested information.
T8 "He's at the store. He'll be home in a little while."	
C8 "O.K."	**C8** Acknowledged comment.

CONVERSATIONAL COMPETENCE EVALUATION
Tucker-Maxon Oral School

Name K.M.   **Age** 5 **Date** 5/12/88

Evaluator Staff

STRUCTURE

Initiation "Hi". "Hi Mom."

Turn Taking Consistent and Contingent.

Ending "Bye". "You're welcome."

FUNCTION

Topic Introduction

Comments "I camping. B. have four puppies."

Requests "I want new car. I go movie?"

Topic Maintenance

Comments "Dog run away fast". "Mommy me go hospital".

"No more bear". "Daddy not home."

Requests "I have puppy?" "I want buy."

Answers "How are you?" "How long?" "How much?" "Why

not?" "Did?" "Where?" "What happened?" "What color?"

"Who?"

Acknowledgements _____ "O.K." "Yeah". "Yes."

_____

Requests Clarification ___ Toy car?

_____

Topical Cohesion

Articles ___ "a"

Pronouns ___ "I"   "my bike"

Ellipsis _____

Extended Turns

Narratives ___ Basic information present.

___ Setting lacks all characters.

___ Problem not clearly stated.

___ Inconsistent use of sentences.

___ No connectors.

_____

_____

Directions ___ Very incomplete.

___ No point of origin statement.

___ Used some locative terms—"over there" "around" "upstairs

___ by"

_____

_____

_____

Explanation List of ingredients _____

 No verbs _____

 Connector—"and" _____

_____

_____

_____

_____

Description Adjectives—"blue, white, yellow" "fast car"

_____

_____

_____

_____

_____

FORM

One-Word Semantic Categories _____

_____

_____

Two-Word Semantic Relationships _____

_____

Three-Word Semantic Relationships Agent—Action—Location/

  Experiencer—Process—Object/Agent—Action—Object

Noun Phrase fast car/new car/four puppies/six day

  grandma(s) house/

Verb Phrase fall (fell)/run (ran)/I (went) camping/have

  (has)/( ) in sleeping bag/I (will) ask/go (to) grandma house/

Negation No more bear/D. not home

Yes/No Questions "I go movie?" "I have puppy?"

WH-Questions "Where daddy?"

Conjoining peanut butter ( ) jam/And jam. And peanut.../

  Mommy ( ) me/And bone.

Relative Clauses

Adverbial Clauses

Noun Clauses _____

_____

Infinitives   ... want ( ) buy _____

_____

Participles   ( ) camping _____

SUMMARY

Structure

Strengths _Good Initiation, Turn-Taking and Ending._

_____

_____

Weaknesses _____

_____

_____

Questions _____

_____

_____

Function

Strengths Good Topic Introduction and Maintenance.

All intents present

Answers wide variety of requests.

Weaknesses Narrative setting incomplete/No use of

sentences/Directions lack origin and limited lexicon/

Explanations lack verbs/Limited pronouns and articles.

Questions _____

_____

_____

_____

Form

Strengths Basic three-word semantic relationships.

Several simple sentences.

Attempts to conjoin and use infinitive.

Weaknesses Limited verb vocabulary and no verb tenses.

No copula or auxiliaries.

Limited locative terms

Questions Additional question forms.

_____

_____

Instructional Objectives

Examining the completed Conversational Competence Evaluation and comparing it with the Stages of Conversational Development it can be seen that this student has acquired the skills and forms of Stage One and needs objectives with focus on developing the skills of Stage Two. Specifically:

1. Initiate conversations with other persons in the school using known routines.
2. Within conversation the student will request information using "What?" and "Where?" questions and three-word yes/no questions with rising intonation.

3. Within conversation the student will produce narratives which include all the characters and locale of the setting.

4. Within conversation the student will produce narratives which include the series of actions using three-word semantic relationships.

5. Within conversation the student will produce explanations which are a series of actions using three-word semantic relationships.

6. Within conversation the student will produce one-step directions which include the verb and locative term.

7. Within conversation the student will produce descriptions which include only distinctive features using an expanded lexicon.

8. Within conversation the student will indicate old information using the pronouns, "he" "she" and "it" and the article, "the."

9. Within conversation the student will indicate new information using the article: a.

10. Within conversation the student will comment using "can't" and "don't."

11. Within conversation the student will introduce topics specified by using a relative clause attached to an indefinite form.'"

12. Within conversation the student will comment using the infinitive form with "have" and "want."

13. Within conversation the student will comment, request and answer using single sentences or extended turns using appropriate past verb forms and present progressive forms with some verbs.

Attainment of these objectives will significantly enhance the student's conversational competence. Once these are attained other conversational skills and forms of Stage Two can be presented.

STUDENT TWO Evaluation Scenario One— Narrative	Comments on Evaluation Scenario One— Narrative
T1 "Pretend that you were riding your bike and a cat ran in front of you. You fell and broke your arm. Your mom took you to the hospital and the doctor put a cast on your arm. Now it's Monday morning and you came to tell me about it."	
C1 "I have cast?"	**C1** Requested clarification.
T2 "Yes, on your arm. You go over there and come into the room.	
C2 "Hi."	**C2** Initiated.
T3 "What happened to you?"	
C3 "I fell my bike. The cat run in front of me."	**C3** Answered request for information. Included locative statement.
T4 "Oh, I sorry. How did that happen?"	

C4 "The cat didn't see me. I didn't see the cat. I fell my bike. I broke my arm. We went to the hospital. Doctor fix cast."	**C4** Answered request for information.
	    Provided incomplete narrative.
	        Setting is incomplete.
	        Lack of connectors.
	        Did not identify person taking him
	            to hospital.
	    Used negative contraction.

T5 "How long will you have to wear it?	
C5 "What?"	**C5** Requested clarification.
T6 "How long will you have the cast?"	
C6 "One month."	**C6** Answered request for information.
T7 "Well, you will have to be more careful."	

C7 "Yeah. I can't ride bike for one month."	**C7** Acknowledged comment.
	    Added comment.
	        Used negative contraction.

STUDENT TWO Evaluation Scenario Two— Narrative	Comments on Evaluation Scenario Two— Narrative
T1 "I am your friend, David, and you are yourself. You went camping with your family. One night you were sleeping and you heard a bear outside. It was trying to get food out of the garbage can. You were all scared. When you come home you tell me all about it. I will be here playing and you come outside."	
C1 "Hi David."	**C1** Initiated conversation.
T2 "Hi."	
C2 "Guess what?"	**C2** Continued initiation.
T3 "What."	
C3 "I went camping. The bear throw garbage can then run away."	**C3** Introduced topic. Provided poorly formed narrative. Setting is incomplete. Problem not clearly stated. Conclusion not stated. Included time connector "then".
T4 "Oh no."	
C4 "Yeah."	**C4** Acknowledged comment.
T5 "Were you scared?"	
C5 "Yeah."	**C5** Answered request for information.
T6 "What did you do?"	
C6 "We go different camp."	**C6** Answered request for information.
T7 "Oh, that was a good idea."	
C7 "I don't like bear."	**C7** Added comment. Used negative contraction.

STUDENT TWO Evaluation Scenario Three— Directions	Comments on Evaluation Scenario Three— Directions
T1 "Now I will be a delivery person and you be Mrs. B. in the office. I will come with some books for the library. I don't know where it is. I will ask you where the library is."	
C1 "O.K."	**C1** Acknowledged understanding of scenario.
T2 "Excuse me. I have some books for the library."	
C2 "O.K."	**C2** Acknowledged comment rather than respond to implied request for information.
T3 "I don't know where it is."	
C3 "I show you where." (Start to get up.)	**C3** Responded to implied request for information. Used noun clause with deleted information i.e., ". . . where."
T4 "Oh, you don't have to show me. Just tell me how to get there."	
C4 "Turn around the corner and open the door. Walk outside. Open door and turn left and turn around the corner. Upstairs library."	**C4** Answered request for information. Provided multi-step directions. Unclear point of origin. Non-specific reference for which door after going outside. Variety of locative terms present.
T5 "Thank you very much."	
C5 "You're welcome."	**C5** Ended appropriately.

STUDENT TWO Evaluation Scenario Four— Explanation	Comments on Evaluation Scenario Four— Explanation
T1 "Let's pretend that it is lunch time. I am your friend, Brian. You have some chocolate chip cookies. They look very good. I'll ask you for one. You give me one and tell me that you made them yourself. I'll ask you how you did that."	
C1 "I make cookies?"	**C1** Requested clarification.
T2 "Yes, and they are delicious."	
C2 "O.K."	**C2** Acknowledged comment.
T3 "Let's start. You be sitting down at the table and I'll come and sit by you."	
C3 "O.K."	**C3** Acknowledged understanding of scenario.
T4 "Hi."	
C4 "Hi."	**C4** Responded to initiation.
T5 "Umm. Those cookies look good. Can I have one?"	
C5 "Here."	**C5** Responded to request for object with action and verbal comment.
T6 "Umm. That is good. Who made it?"	
C6 "I make cookies."	**C6** Answered request for information.
T7 "How did you do that."	
C7 "Put in milk, eggs and powder. Stir and stir. Put cookies in oven. Wait. Take out."	**C7** Answered request for information. Provided explanation. Included list of ingredients. Included sequence of actions with appropriate verbs. Some details missing. Lack of connectors.
T8 "Wow, you are a good cook."	
C8 "You want more cookie?"	**C8** Requested information. Omitted auxiliary.
T9 "Sure. Thank you."	
C9 "You're welcome."	**C9** Ended appropriately.

STUDENT TWO Evaluation Scenario Five— Description	Comments on Evaluation Scenario Five— Description
T1 "Now let's pretend that I am your Mom. You went to the store with your friends. You saw a motorcycle that you want to buy. You come home and tell me about it and ask me if you can have it."	
C1 "O.K."	**C1** Acknowledged understanding of scenario.
T2 "I'll be in the kitchen and you come in and talk to me."	
C2 (Pretends to be opening front door. Calls.) "Mom."	**C2** Initiated conversation.
T3 "Hi, did you have fun at the store."	
C3 "Yeah. I saw motorcycle. I like to buy a motorcycle."	**C3** Answered request for information. Introduced topic by commenting. Used infinitive.
T4 "A motorcycle! What does it look like?"	
C4 "Yellow. It got motor. Can I buy motorcycle?"	**C4** Answered request for information. Provided inadequate description. Request information. Included auxiliary.
T5 "I don't know. How much does it cost?"	
C5 "Two hundred dollar."	**C5** Answered request for information.
T6 "Wow. That's a lot of money. We'll see."	
C6 "I like yellow motorcycle."	**C6** Added comment.

STUDENT TWO Evaluation Scenario Six— Description	Comments on Evaluation Scenario Six— Description
T1 "Pretend that one day you were walking to school and you saw someone stealing a bicycle. You call the police to tell them. I'll be the policeman."	
C1 "O.K."	**C1** Acknowledged understanding of scenario.
T2 "Let's start."	
C2 (To himself) "Oh no. Steal the bike. I call the police." (Pretends to dial a telephone.) "Ring. Ring."	**C2** Commented.
T3 "Hello. This is the police department."	
C3 "Hello police. The boy took my friend's bike."	**C3** Responded to initiation. Introduced topic by commenting. Inappropriate article.
T4 "What did he look like?"	
C4 "He have brown hair and green shirt and he wear brown pants."	**C4** Answered request for information. Provided organized description. Included body and clothing features. Used "and" as only connector.
T5 "How old was he?"	
C5 "I think he twelve year old."	**C5** Answered request for information. Used noun clause.
T6 "What did the bike look like?"	
C6 "Blue and black wheel and black seat."	**C6** Answered request for information. Provided description. Used "and" as connector.
T7 "O.K. We will look for the bike and the boy. Thank you for calling."	
C7 "You're welcome."	**C7** Ended appropriately.

STUDENT TWO Evaluation Scenario Seven— Conversation	Comments on Evaluation Scenario Seven— Conversation
T1 "This time I am going to be your friend, Josh. I am going to call you on the phone to see if you can go to a movie. You have to ask your Mom. I'll be your Mom, too."	
C1 "O.K."	**C1** Acknowledged understanding of scenario.
T2 "Ring. Ring."	
C2 "Hello."	**C2** Initiated appropriately.
T3 "Hi, this is Josh."	
C3 "Hi Josh."	**C3** Responded to initiation.
T4 "Can you go to a movie tonight?"	
C4 "I don't know. I ask my Mom."	**C4** Answered request for information. Used negative contraction. Commented.
T5 "O.K."	
C5 (To Mom) "Mom, can I go movie tonight?"	**C5** Initiated new conversation. Introduced topic by requesting information. Placed auxiliary in correct position. Omitted location term.
T6 (As Mom) "Oh I'm sorry. You can't go because we are going to grandma's house for dinner."	
C6 "Oh. I tell Josh."	**C6** Acknowledged comment. Added comment.
C7 "Josh, I can't go movie with you."	**C7** Re-initiated conversation. Completed answer to request for information. Used negative contraction. Omitted locative term.

STUDENT TWO Evaluation Scenario Seven— Conversation cont'd	Comments on Evaluation Scenario Seven— Conversation cont'd
T7 "Why not?" **C8** "I have to go grandma for eat dinner."	**C8** Answered request for information. Used infinitive. Omitted locative term Used "for" in place of "to" in infinitive.
T8 "Oh well. Maybe we can go next week." **C9** "O.K."	**C9** Answered implied request for information.
T9 "Bye." **C10** "Bye."	**C10** Ended appropriately.

STUDENT TWO Evaluation Scenario Eight— Conversation	Comments on Evaluation Scenario Eight— Conversation
T1 "I'm going to be your Mom. You went over to Eric's house. He has some new puppies. You want to have one so you come home and ask me if you can have one. I'll be reading a book in the living room and you come in the house." **C1** "Hi, Mom."	**C1** Initiated appropriately.
T2 "Hi. Did you have fun at Eric's house?" **C2** "Yes. Eric have new puppies."	**C2** Answered request for information. Commented.
T3 "Oh, how nice." **C3** "I want puppy."	**C3** Requested object.
T4 "Well, do you know how to take care of a puppy?"	

STUDENT TWO Evaluation Scenario Eight— Conversation cont'd	Comments on Evaluation Scenario Eight— Conversation cont'd
C4 "Yes. I take care puppy."	C4 Answered request for information.
T5 "What will you do?"	
C5 "Go the park and play and sleep my bedroom."	C5 Answered request for information. Omitted locative terms.
T6 "Is that all. Just play with it?"	
C6 "I give dog food and dog house."	C6 Answered request for information.
T7 "Hmmm. I don't know. What do they look like?"	
C7 "Brown and white with the spots."	C7 Answered request for information. Provided description. Used "with" phrase. Inappropriate use of article.
T8 "Well they sound cute. I guess you can have one."	
C8 "I get puppy now."	C8 Commented.
T9 "O.K." Bring it right back. I want to see it."	
C9 "O.K."	C9 Acknowledged request for action

CONVERSATIONAL COMPETENCE EVALUATION

Tucker-Maxon Oral School

Name __G.S.__ Age __14__ Date __5/11/88__

Evaluator __P.F.__

STRUCTURE

Initiation __"Hi". "Guess what". "Mom."__

Turn-Taking   Consistently contingent.

Ending   "O.K." "You're welcome."

FUNCTION

Topic Introduction

Comments   "I went camping". "I saw motorcycle". "Eric have

puppies."

Requests   "Can I go movie?"

Topic Maintenance

Comments

Requests   "I want puppy". "You want more cookie?" "Can

I buy?"

Answers   "Were you ...?" "What did ... do?" "Who ...?"

"When ...?" "How long ...?" "What happened?" "Why not?"

"What ...?"

Acknowledgements   "O.K." "Yeah."

Requests Clarification   "I have cast?" "What?" "I make

cookies?"

Topical Cohesion

Articles _Uses 'the' for new information._

Pronouns _Inconsistent_

Ellipsis

Extended Turns

Narratives _Settings not complete._

Lack of connectors.

Gives series of actions using simple sentences

Directions _No origin statement._

Uses variety of locative terms—around, left, upstairs.

Lacks specificity.

Explanation _List of ingredients and appropriate verbs._

Some details missing.

Needs connectors.

Description   Good description of thief—physical features and

clothes.

Uses color words

Good description of puppies—'brown and white with the

    spots'

FORM

One-Word Semantic Categories

Two-Word Semantic Relationships

Three-Word Semantic Relationships

Noun Phrase   "... my friend's bike ..."/"two hundred dollars"/

"(the)" hospital/"

Verb Phrase _"fell (off)"/"go (went)"/"go (to) movie"/"I ask"/_

"throw (threw)"/"... take care (of) ..."/"open the door"/"he

wear/"

Negation _"didn't see"/"I can't"/"I don't know"/"... don't_

like ..."

Yes/No Questions _"Can I buy ...?" "Can I go ...?" "(Do) you_

want more ...?"

WH-Questions _"What?"_

Conjoining _"... and ..."/"... then run ..."/_

Relative Clauses

Adverbial Clauses

Noun Clauses _"I show you where". "I think he twelve ..."_

Infinitives _"I like to buy". "I have to go (to) ..." "for (to)_

eat ..."

Participles

SUMMARY

Structure

Strengths <u>All aspects o.k.</u>

_____

_____

Weaknesses _____

_____

_____

Questions _____

_____

_____

Function

Strengths <u>Good Topic Introduction and Maintenance</u>

<u>Explanation is good. Description is good.</u>

_____

<u>Answers wide variety of question types</u>

Weaknesses <u>Narratives have incomplete settings and lack</u>

<u>connectors.</u>

<u>No origin in Directions.</u>

_____

Questions _____

_____

_____

_____

Form

Strengths _Consistent use of simple sentences._

Several attempts of complex sentences.

_____

Weaknesses _Inconsistent verb tense. Inconsistent_

conjoining. Lack of auxiliaries in comments and questions.

Questions _____

_____

_____

Instructional Objectives

Comparing the Conversational Evaluation with the Stages of Conversational Development indicates that this student has attained most of the skills and forms of Stage Two and some of Stage Three e.g. "Guess what." Some Stage Two items, including relative clauses and WH-questions, do not appear in the sample, so the teacher will want to carry out some test scenarios to determine what level of skill the student has and add those to the list of objectives if appropriate. The following objectives are drawn from Stage Three.

1. Within conversation the student will request information using "Am" and "Are" yes/no questions with the auxiliary inverted.
2. Within conversation the student will request information using "Why" and "How" questions.
3. Within conversation the student will request clarification using the expression "Pardon me."
4. Within conversation the student will produce narratives which include all elements of the setting.

5. Within conversation the student will produce narratives which include use of the time connector "Then."

6. Within conversation the student will produce directions which have a clear point of origin.

7. Within conversation the student will produce explanations which include an organizing statement and time connectors.

8. Within conversation the student will produce descriptions which include "with phrases."

9. Within conversation the student will consistently use pronouns and "the" to signal old information.

10. Within conversation the student will use "a" to signal new information.

Additional skill and skill/form objectives will need to be attained before this student is ready to move to Stage Four. However, attaining these objectives will bring about a substantial increase in this student's conversational competence.

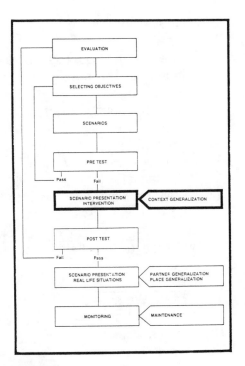

15 Appendix B

**This Appendix presents additional examples of
Scenario Presentation and Intervention.**

Example One

This scenario was designed to help this student increase his skill
of including all the characters within the setting of a narrative. The
interventions are underlined.

T: "Let's pretend that you spent the weekend with your
grandma and grandpa. On Saturday you went to the zoo.
You saw lots of animals and watched the zookeeper feed
the lions. Then you rode the train and ate hot dogs. On
Monday you come in and tell me about it."

C: "O.K." (Walks to door and pretends to come in.) "Hi."

T: "Hi."

C: "Guess what."

T: "What?"

C: "I went to the zoo. I saw bears and lions and giraffe and elephants. The man give food to lions. I ride the train. I eat hot dogs.

T: "Boy, that sounds like fun."

C: "Yeah."

T: "Let's switch."

T: (As child) "You know what?"

C: (As teacher) "No."

T: "Well, on Saturday I went to the zoo with my grandma and grandpa. I saw bears, monkeys, giraffes, penguins and lions. We watched the zookeeper feed the lions. Then we rode on the train. After that we had hot dogs and cokes."

C: "You have fun."

T: "Yeah. We sure did."

T: "Let's start over."

C: "Guess what."

T: "What?"

C: "I went to the zoo with my grandma and grandpa. I saw monkeys, bears, elephants, tigers and lions. The zookeeper feed the lions. I ride the train. I eat hot dogs and drink pop."

T: "Oh. wow. That sounds like fun. You sure have nice grand-parents."

C: "Yeah.

In this scenario the student needed only one role switch to include his grandparents in the setting of narrative. Continued practice with narrative scenarios will further enhance his ability. It is interesting to note that on his second attempt he used "zookeeper" instead of "man".

Sometimes kids think previous has 'man' was not right or okay to use in this case.

Example Two

The following scenario was designed to help a student achieve the objective of giving directions which begin with a clear point of origin.

T: "Let's pretend that I am a visitor to school. I come in the front door and see you walking to the office. I want to see

Mrs. S. I don't know where her room is. I'll ask you for help."

C: "I going to office?"

T: "Yes, your teacher wants you to get some paper."

C: "Oh."

T: "You go over there and pretend you're walking to the office. I'll come in the door and talk to you."

C: "O.K."

T: (As visitor) "Pardon me, I'm looking for Mrs. S.'s room. Can you tell me how to get there?"

C: "Yes. Go over there. Open the door. Turn left. Go to room.

T: "Let's switch. You be the visitor and I'll be you."

C: (As visitor) "Pardon me. Where is Mrs. S.'s room?"

T: (As student) "Go down this hall and go out the door. Go into the other building. Turn left and go to the second door. That's her room."

C: "Thank you."

T: "Let's switch back."

T: (As visitor) "Excuse me. I'm supposed to visit Mrs. S. Can you tell me where her room is?"

C: "Yes. Go over there. Go outside to gym. Open the door. Turn left. Go to second door."

T: "Let's switch again."

C: (As visitor) "Pardon me. Where is Mrs. S.'s room?"

T: (As student) "Go down this hall. Go out the door and go to the other building. Turn left and go to the second door."

C: "Thank you."

T: "Let's switch back."

T: (As visitor) "Excuse me. I'm looking for Mrs. S.'s room. Can you tell me where it is?"

C: "Sure. Go this hall. Go outside. Go to gym. Open the door. Turn left and go to second door."

T: "Thank you."

C: "You're welcome."

desired goal

Two role switches were necessary before this student improved his ability to specify the point of origin of his directions. There are other skills he needs to acquire to make his direction giving complete which will be covered in future scenarios.

Example Three

The following scenario was designed to help a student acquire the ability to acknowledge the comments of others. This is a Stage One objective that is important for young children to achieve.

T: "Let's pretend that I am mom. You are P. We are driving to school. (Arranges two chairs to simulate a front seat. Pretends to be driving.)

C: "School?"

T: "We are in the car. We are driving to school." (Pretends to be holding the steering wheel and driving.)

C: "(Sits and pretends to be looking out the window.)

T: (As Mom) "Oh look at that big tree."

C: (Looks but makes no acknowledgement.)

T: "Let's switch." (Teacher and child switch seats to assist child in assuming new role.)

C: (As Mom, pretends to be driving) "Tree. Big."

T: (As child) "Yeah." (Nods head.) "It's big."

T: "Let's switch back." (Teacher and child exchange seats and roles.)

T: (As Mom) "Oh look at that big tree."

C: (Looks but remains silent.)

T: "Let's switch." (Both switch seats and roles.)

C: (As Mom, pretends to drive) "Tree. Big."

T: (As child, vigorously nods head) "Yeah. A big tree."

T: "Let's switch back." (Teacher and child exchange seats and roles.

T: (As Mom) "Oh look at that big tree."

C: "Yeah." (Nods head)

T: "Oh, here we are at school. I'll see you later."

C: "Bye."

T: "Bye."

After two role switches this child was able to acknowledge the comment of his Mom. This and the other topic introduction and maintenance skills are critical for children to acquire at an early stage. With one-word utterances children can engage in meaningful conversations if they have the proper skills. These skills will make it more likely that other persons will be able to engage them in conversation because their skills will allow participation.

Example Four

This scenario was designed to help a student acquire the ability to comment using a relative clause to specify a particular person.

T: "Let's pretend that I am your Mom and we are at home. Last week a dog came in our yard and bit your brother, Rick. Today you were playing outside and you saw that dog. You come in to tell me about it."

C: "O.K." (Walks to door and pretends to come in.) "Mom! Mom!"

T: (As Mom) What?"

C: "I was playing outside. I saw the dog."

T: "You saw the dog. What dog?"

C: "You remember. He came in our yard and bit Rick's leg."

T: "Oh, you saw the dog that bit Rick's leg."(Teacher Clarification).

C: "Yes."

T: "Let's start over."

C: "Mom!"

T: "What?"

C: "I was playing outside. I saw the dog bit Rick's leg."

T: "Oh! You saw the dog that bit Rick's leg."(Teacher Clarification).

C: "Yes. He's outside in our yard."

T: "Let's start over."

C: "Mom!"

T: "What?"

C: "I was playing outside. I saw the dog that bit Rick's leg."

T: "Oh. Let's go find him right now."

C: "O.K."

In this case the teacher had been working on relative clauses for a time and felt that with Teacher Clarification the student would improve her production. After the first Clarification the student did come close to an acceptable statement. This improvement encourage the teacher to continue with the strategy. The result was an appropriate relative clause after the second Clarification.

16 Appendix C

Christine Soland

This Appendix presents ideas for implementing individualized instruction in the classroom. Developing conversational competence is best achieved when the teacher is able to work individually with each child. The ideas contained here will assist the the teacher who is unfamiliar with strategies for individualizing instruction.

INDIVIDUALIZING INSTRUCTION

Since acquisition of conversational competence is unique for each child, it is necessary for the classroom teacher to individualize objectives and instruction. Even when two or more children have very similar needs it is highly likely that individual differences in learning style and experience will necessitate variation in objectives, content of scenarios, and intervention strategies. Therefore, a one-to-one conversational instruction period for each child in the class needs to be part of the daily routine. In this way each child will achieve to his or her maximum potential.

Learning Centers

In order to individualize instruction it is necessary to create learning centers and manage instruction around them. There are three types of learning centers:

1. The teacher center.
2. The teacher aid center.
3. The child center.

Teacher Center: Here the teacher implements the one-to-one instructional model. All steps of the model are carried out at this center. In classes where numbers of children are large and/or space is limited one student may be engaged watching another student work with the teacher.

Teacher Aid Center: Here the teacher aid works with one or two children. The number of children will depend on total numbers of children in the room and available resources for the Child Centers. The aid can play learning games with the students, review previously taught material, work on spelling or vocabulary, re-enact scenarios to achieve partner generalization or carry on any number of activities.

Child Centers: Here the children work independently at various tasks intended to solidify previous learning, expand knowledge or develop increased skills. Some activities that have been found useful and productive include:

1. Listening to stories on tape recorders or language masters.
2. Developing specific listening skills using language masters.
3. Viewing filmstrips and answering questions.
4. Completing math problems.
5. Completing science observations and recording data.
6. Practicing penmanship.
7. Writing stories.
8. Completing puzzles and learning games.
9. Assigned and/or free reading.
10. Working at a computer.

Classroom Arrangement

The placement of learning centers in the classroom is critical to their success. Each should be spaced far enough from the others so that the activity at each doesn't interfere with others. In this way children have room to work and not disturb others. Sufficient counter space is needed for student records and files. All materials needed by children should be easily accessible at each center.

Learning centers can be located anywhere in the room or outside the room. They can be in the hall outside the classroom door or in a closet. They can be under a table or in a large box. A reading center can be created with a book shelf and some large pillows on the floor.

Scheduling

Learning Centers are run on a schedule. Children rotate through each learning center for a specific amount of time. They know the sequence of rotation and they understand how the beginning and end of each rotation is signaled. Children can be given a personal schedule or a master schedule can be posted in the conspicuous location.

Presented below is a sample schedule for a class with six children, a teacher and a teacher aide.

Schedule						
Time	8:45	9:00	9:15	9:30	9:45	10:00
S. One	Filmstrip	Math Book	Aid	Language Master	Teacher	Read
S. Two	Read	Filmstrip	Math Book	Aid	Language Master	Teacher
S. Three	Teacher	Read	Filmstrip	Math Book	Aid	Language Master
S. Four	Language Master	Teacher	Read	Filmstrip	Math Book	Aid
S. Five	Aid	Language Master	Teacher	Read	Filmstrip	Math Book
S. Six	Math Book	Aid	Language Master	Teacher	Read	Filmstrip

Following this schedule each child will work with the teacher on conversational skills for fifteen minutes and have fifteen minutes to re-do old scenarios with the teacher aid. Notice that the schedule has the students work with the teacher and teacher aid spread out during the morning.

Alternative Scheduling

In cases where no teacher aid is available the teacher could have the student scheduled for the aid in the above schedule to observe another student working on scenarios.

If seven children are in the room doubling up the studer's working with the teacher aid is a good alternative.

If eight children are in the room doubling up both the teacher and teacher aid are effective.

Learning Centers and Autonomy

Managing a classroom with learning centers has many benefits. Most importantly they give the teacher time to work with each child individually to develop his or her conversational competence. Learning centers also give children the opportunity to think and act for themselves. When children do this they are developing their autonomy.

At learning centers children are responsible for themselves rather than having to rely on a teacher to tell them what to do. They act on learning center objects and make decisions about their actions by themselves. When children are allowed to work independently, they are removed from direct adult control. They set up their own rules and develop a respect for their own values, thoughts and feelings. Perhaps, children even work harder trying to achieve learning goals they have established for themselves.

17 Bibliography

Applebee, A.N. (1978). *The Child's Concept of Story*. Chicago, IL: University of Chicago Press.

Bates, E. (1976). *Language and Context: The Acquisition of Pragmatics*. New York, NY: Academic Press.

Bloom, L. and Lahey, M. (1978). *Language Development and Language Disorders*. New York, NY: John Wiley & Sons.

Brown, R. (1979). *A First Language*. Cambridge, MA: Harvard University Press.

Bruner, J.S. (1975). "The ontogensis of speech acts" *Journal of Child Language*. pp. 2, 1–19.

Bruner, J.S. (1978). "Firm communication to language: A psychological perspective" in I. Markova (ed) *The Social Context of Language*. New York, NY: John Wiley & Sons.

Clark, H. and Clark E. (1977). *Psychology and Language*. New York, NY: Harcourt, Brace, Jovanovitch.

Cazden, C. (1979). "Peekaboo as an instructional model: Discourse development at home and school" *Papers and Reports on Child Language Development*. pp. 17, 1–29.

Dore, J. (1979). "Conversation and preschool language development" in Fletcher and Garman (eds) *Language Acquisition*. Cambridge, MA: Cambridge University Press.

Ervin-Tripp, S. (1977). "From conversation to syntax" *Papers and Reports on Child Language Development*. pp 13, 11–21.

Flavell, J. (1971). "Stage-related properties of cognitive development" *Cognitive Psychology*. pp. 2, 421–453.

Foster, S. H. (1982). "Learning to develop a topic" *Papers and Reports on Child Language Development*. p. 21.

Foster, S. H. (1983). "Topic and the development of discourse structure" in Truax and Schultz (eds) *Learning to Communicate*. Washington D.C.: A. G. Bell Association for the Deaf.

Grice, H. P. (1975). "Logic and conversation" in Cole and Morgan (eds) *Syntax and Semantics*. New York, NY: Academic Press.

Guess, D., Keogh, W. and Sailor, W. (1978). Generalization of speech and language behavior" in Schiefelbusch (ed) *Bases of Language Intervention*. Baltimore, MD: University Park Press.

Halliday, M. A. and Hasan, R. (1976). *Cohesion in English*. London: Longmans.

Keller-Cohen, D. (1978). "Context in child language" in Siegel, Beals and Tyler (eds) *Annual Review of Anthropology*. pp. 7, 453–482.

Kretschmer R. and Kretschmer, L. (1978). *Language Development and Intervention with the Hearing-Impaired*. Baltimore, MD: University Park Press.

Kretschmer, R. and Kretschmer, L. (1980). "Pragmatics: Development in normal hearing and hearing-impaired children's" in Subtelny, (ed) *Speech Assessment and Speech Improvement for the Hearing-Impaired*. Washington, D.C.: A. G. Bell Association for the Deaf.

Kretschmer R. (1981). "Reaction to seven and eight" in Mulholland (ed) *Oral Education: Today and Tomorrow*. Washington, D.C.: A. G. Bell Association for the Deaf.

Lee, L. (1974). *Development Sentence Analysis*. Evanston, IL: Northwestern University Press.

Ling, D. (1976). *Speech and the Hearing-Impaired Child*. Washington, D.C.: A. G. Bell Association for the Deaf.

Lund, N. J. and Duchan, J. F. (1983). *Assessing Children's Lan-*

guage in Naturalistic Contexts. Englewood Cliffs, N.J.: Prentice-Hall, Inc.

Mandler, J. M. and Johnson, N. S. (1977). "Rememberance of things parsed: Story structure and recall" *Cognitive Psychology.* pp. 9, 111–115.

McKirdy, L. S. and Blank, M. (1982). "Dialogue in deaf and hearing pre-schoolers" *Journal of Speech and Hearing Research.* pp. 25, 487–499.

Miller, J. (1981). *Assessing Language Production in Children.* Baltimore, MD: University Park Press.

Mishler, E. G. (1979). "Meaning in context: Is there any other kind?" *Harvard Educational Review.* pp 49, 1–19.

Moog, J. S. and Geers, A. (1979). *Grammatical Analysis of Elicited Language.* St. Louis, MO: Central Institute for the Deaf.

Nelson, K. (1981). "Individual differences in language development: Implications for development and language" *Developmental Psychology.* pp. 17, 170–187.

Popham, W. J. and Baker, E. (1970). *Systematic Instruction.* Englewood Cliffs, N. J.: Prentice-Hall, Inc.

Prutting, C. A. (1982). "Pragmatics and social competence" *Journal of Speech and Hearing Disorders.* pp. 47, 123–134.

Quigley, S., Steinkamp, M., Power, D. and Jones, B. (1978). *Test of Syntactic Abilities.* Beaverton, OR.: Dormac.

Rumelhart, D. E. (1975). "Notes on a schema for stories" in Babrow and Collins (eds) *Representation and Understanding.* New York, NY: Academic Press.

Sadow, M. W. (1982). "The use of story grammar in the design of questions" *The Reading Teacher.* pp. 35, 5, 19–22.

Snow, C. and Ferguson, C. (eds) (1977). *Talking to Children.* Cambridge, MA: Cambridge University Press.

Stein, N. L. (1978). *How Children Understand Stories: A Developmental Analysis.* Champaign, IL.: University of Illinois at Urbana-Champaign Press.

Stein, N. L. and Glenn, C. G. (1979). "An analysis of story comprehension in elementary school children" in Freedle (ed) *New Directions in Discourse Processing.* Norwood, N.J.: Ablex.

Stokes, T. F. and Baer, T. M. (1977). "An implicit technology of generalization" *Journal of Applied Behavior Analysis.* pp. 10, 349–367.

Waterson, N. and Snow C. (eds) (1978). *The Development of Communication.* New York, NY: John Wiley & Sons.

NOTES